FOR THE WELL-BEING OF ALL

FOR THE WELL-BEING OF ALL

Eliminating the Extremes
of Wealth and Poverty

Compiled by Bonnie J. Taylor

BAHÁ'Í
PUBLISHING

WILMETTE, ILLINOIS

Bahá'í Publishing
401 Greenleaf Avenue, Wilmette, Illinois 60091

23 22 21 20   4 3 2 1

Library of Congress Cataloging in Publication Control Number:
2020040586

Cover design by Carlos Esparza
Book design by Patrick Falso

CONTENTS

INTRODUCTION

This compilation offers a selection of passages on one of the key aims of the Bahá'í Faith—the elimination of the extremes of wealth and poverty on a global scale. The selections gathered here, taken from Bahá'í scripture and other Bahá'í sources, present the vision of a just and unified global civilization that is both materially and spiritually prosperous. Achieving such a vision requires individual and collective transformation, based on learning over time and through experience how to put spiritual principles into practice. This work offers a collection of passages setting out such principles and related guidance, along with a brief description of how the worldwide Bahá'í community is currently engaged in learning to advance economic justice at the grassroots level.

The Bahá'í Faith is an independent world religion founded in Persia (present-day Iran) in 1844. In the words of Shoghi Effendi, the appointed head of the Faith from 1921 until 1957, the Faith

> . . . upholds the unity of God, recognizes the unity of His Prophets, and inculcates the principle of the oneness and wholeness of the entire human race. It proclaims the necessity and the inevitability of the unification of mankind, asserts that it is gradually approaching, and claims that nothing short of the transmuting spirit of God, working through His chosen Mouthpiece in this day, can ultimately succeed in bringing it about. It, moreover, enjoins upon its followers the primary duty of an unfettered search after truth, condemns all manner of prejudice and superstition, declares the purpose of religion to be the promotion of amity and concord, proclaims its essential harmony with science, and

recognizes it as the foremost agency for the pacification and the orderly progress of human society.

The Faith's scripture is comprised of the writings of its Prophet-Founder Bahá'u'lláh (1817–92); His forerunner and Prophet-Herald, the Báb (1819–1950); and His son and appointed successor 'Abdu'l-Bahá (1844–1921). Their writings, along with those of Shoghi Effendi and the Universal House of Justice, are considered authoritative by Bahá'ís. The House of Justice is the elected international governing body of the Bahá'í global community and an institution ordained in the writings of Bahá'u'lláh. Selections from other sources in this work, such as those of international agencies of the Faith, while not authoritative, are included for the insight they offer into the application of these teachings.

It is to a message of the Universal House of Justice, addressed to the Bahá'ís of the world in March 2017, that we first turn, as it effectively frames the content that follows. This letter provides invaluable insight into the state of the modern world and offers a broad glimpse of the Bahá'í perspective on the nature of global economics, as well as our role as individual participants in economic systems.

LETTER REGARDING ECONOMIC LIFE FROM THE UNIVERSAL HOUSE OF JUSTICE

In an increasingly interconnected world, more light is being cast on the social conditions of every people, giving greater visibility to their circumstances. While there are developments that give hope, there is much that should weigh heavy on the conscience of the human race. Inequity, discrimination, and exploitation blight the life of humanity, seemingly immune to the treatments applied by political schemes of every hue. The economic impact of these afflictions has resulted in the prolonged suffering of so many, as well as in deep-seated, structural defects in society. No one whose heart has been attracted to the teachings of the Blessed Beauty can remain unmoved by these consequences. "The world is in great turmoil," Bahá'u'lláh observes in the Lawḥ-i-Dunyá, "and the minds of its people are in a state of utter confusion. We entreat the Almighty that He may graciously illuminate them with the glory of His Justice, and enable them to discover that which will be profitable unto them at all times and under all conditions." As the Bahá'í community strives to contribute at the level of thought and action to the betterment of the world, the adverse conditions experienced by many populations will more and more demand its attention.

The welfare of any segment of humanity is inextricably bound up with the welfare of the whole. Humanity's collective life suffers when any one group thinks of its own well-being in isolation from that of its neighbours or pursues economic gain without regard for how the natural environment, which provides sustenance for all, is affected. A stubborn obstruction, then, stands in the way of meaningful social progress: time and again, avarice and self-interest prevail at the expense of the common good. Unconscionable

1

quantities of wealth are being amassed, and the instability this creates is made worse by how income and opportunity are spread so unevenly both between nations and within nations. But it need not be so. However much such conditions are the outcome of history, they do not have to define the future, and even if current approaches to economic life satisfied humanity's stage of adolescence, they are certainly inadequate for its dawning age of maturity. There is no justification for continuing to perpetuate structures, rules, and systems that manifestly fail to serve the interests of all peoples. The teachings of the Faith leave no room for doubt: there is an inherent moral dimension to the generation, distribution, and utilization of wealth and resources.

The stresses emerging out of the long-term process of transition from a divided world to a united one are being felt within international relations as much as in the deepening fractures that affect societies large and small. With prevailing modes of thought found to be badly wanting, the world is in desperate need of a shared ethic, a sure framework for addressing the crises that gather like storm clouds. The vision of Bahá'u'lláh challenges many of the assumptions that are allowed to shape contemporary discourse—for instance, that self-interest, far from needing to be restrained, drives prosperity, and that progress depends upon its expression through relentless competition. To view the worth of an individual chiefly in terms of how much one can accumulate and how many goods one can consume relative to others is wholly alien to Bahá'í thought. But neither are the teachings in sympathy with sweeping dismissals of wealth as inherently distasteful or immoral, and asceticism is prohibited. Wealth must serve humanity. Its use must accord with spiritual principles; systems must be created in their light. And, in Bahá'u'lláh's memorable words, "No light can compare with the light of justice. The establishment of order in the world and the tranquility of the nations depend upon it."

Although Bahá'u'lláh does not set out in His Revelation a detailed economic system, a constant theme throughout the entire corpus of His teachings is the reorganization of human society. Consideration of this theme

2

inevitably gives rise to questions of economics. Of course, the future order conceived by Bahá'u'lláh is far beyond anything that can be imagined by the present generation. Nevertheless, its eventual emergence will depend on strenuous effort by His followers to put His teachings into effect today. With this in mind, we hope that the comments below will stimulate thoughtful, ongoing reflection by the friends. The aim is to learn about how to participate in the material affairs of society in a way that is consistent with the divine precepts and how, in practical terms, collective prosperity can be advanced through justice and generosity, collaboration and mutual assistance.

Our call to examine the implications of the Revelation of Bahá'u'lláh for economic life is intended to reach Bahá'í institutions and communities but is directed more especially to the individual believer. If a new model of community life, patterned on the teachings, is to emerge, must not the company of the faithful demonstrate in their own lives the rectitude of conduct that is one of its most distinguishing features? Every choice a Bahá'í makes—as employee or employer, producer or consumer, borrower or lender, benefactor or beneficiary—leaves a trace, and the moral duty to lead a coherent life demands that one's economic decisions be in accordance with lofty ideals, that the purity of one's aims be matched by the purity of one's actions to fulfil those aims. Naturally, the friends habitually look to the teachings to set the standard to which to aspire. But the community's deepening engagement with society means that the economic dimension of social existence must receive ever more concentrated attention. Particularly in clusters where the community-building process is beginning to embrace large numbers, the exhortations contained in the Bahá'í Writings should increasingly inform economic relationships within families, neighbourhoods, and peoples. Not content with whatever values prevail in the existing order that surrounds them, the friends everywhere should consider the application of the teachings to their lives and, using the opportunities their circumstances offer them, make their own individual and collective contributions to economic justice and social progress wherever they reside. Such efforts will add to a growing storehouse of knowledge in this regard.

A foundational concept to explore in this context is the spiritual reality of man. In the Revelation of Bahá'u'lláh, the nobility inherent to every human being is unequivocally asserted; it is a fundamental tenet of Bahá'í belief, upon which hope for the future of humankind is built. The soul's capacity to manifest all the names and attributes of God—He Who is the Compassionate, the Bestower, the Bountiful—is repeatedly affirmed in the Writings. Economic life is an arena for the expression of honesty, integrity, trustworthiness, generosity, and other qualities of the spirit. The individual is not merely a self-interested economic unit, striving to claim an ever-greater share of the world's material resources. "Man's merit lieth in service and virtue," Bahá'u'lláh avers, "and not in the pageantry of wealth and riches." And further: "Dissipate not the wealth of your precious lives in the pursuit of evil and corrupt affection, nor let your endeavours be spent in promoting your personal interest." By consecrating oneself to the service of others, one finds meaning and purpose in life and contributes to the upliftment of society itself. At the outset of His celebrated treatise *The Secret of Divine Civilization*, 'Abdu'l-Bahá states:

> And the honor and distinction of the individual consist in this, that he among all the world's multitudes should become a source of social good. Is any larger bounty conceivable than this, that an individual, looking within himself, should find that by the confirming grace of God he has become the cause of peace and well-being, of happiness and advantage to his fellow men? No, by the one true God, there is no greater bliss, no more complete delight.

Viewed in this light, many seemingly ordinary economic activities gain new significance because of their potential to add to human welfare and prosperity. "Every person must have an occupation, a trade or a craft," explains the Master, "so that he may carry other people's burdens, and not himself be a burden to others." The poor are urged by Bahá'u'lláh to "exert themselves and strive to earn the means of livelihood," while they who are possessed of riches "must have the utmost regard for the poor." "Wealth," 'Abdu'l-Bahá has affirmed, "is praiseworthy in the highest degree, if it is acquired by an individual's own efforts and the grace of God, in commerce, agriculture, art and industry, and if it be expended for philanthropic purposes." At the same time, the Hidden Words is replete with warnings of its perilous allure, that wealth is a "mighty barrier" between the believer and the proper Object of his adoration. No wonder, then, that Bahá'u'lláh extols the station of the wealthy one who is not hindered by riches from attaining the eternal kingdom; the splendour of such a soul "shall illuminate the dwellers of heaven even as the sun enlightens the people of the earth!" 'Abdu'l-Bahá declares that "if a judicious and resourceful individual should initiate measures which would universally enrich the masses of the people, there could be no undertaking greater than this, and it would rank in the sight of God as the supreme achievement." For wealth is most commendable "provided the entire population is wealthy." Examining one's life to determine what is a necessity and then discharging with joy one's obligation in relation to the law of Ḥuqúqu'lláh* is an indispensable discipline to bring one's priorities into balance, purify whatever wealth one possesses, and ensure that the share which is the Right of God provides for the greater good. At all times, contentment and moderation, benevolence and fellow feeling, sacrifice and reliance on the Almighty are qualities that befit the God-fearing soul.

The forces of materialism promote a quite contrary line of thinking: that happiness comes from constant acquisition, that the more one has the better, that worry for the environment is for another day. These seductive messages

---

* Ḥuqúqu'lláh, meaning *the Right of God,* is one of the fundamental ordinances of the Bahá'í Faith, and a law and institution established by Bahá'u'lláh. The law prescribes that each Bahá'í shall pay a certain portion of his accumulated savings after the deduction of all necessary expenses and of certain exempt properties such as one's residence. These payments provide a fund at the disposition of the head of the Faith for carrying out beneficent activities. Ḥuqúqu'lláh is administered by the Universal House of Justice, and payments are made to trustees appointed by the Universal House of Justice in every country or region.

fuel an increasingly entrenched sense of personal entitlement, which uses the language of justice and rights to disguise self-interest. Indifference to the hardship experienced by others becomes commonplace while entertainment and distracting amusements are voraciously consumed. The enervating influence of materialism seeps into every culture, and all Bahá'ís recognize that, unless they strive to remain conscious of its effects, they may to one degree or another unwittingly adopt its ways of seeing the world. Parents must be acutely aware that, even when very young, children absorb the norms of their surroundings. The junior youth spiritual empowerment programme encourages thoughtful discernment at an age when the call of materialism grows more insistent. With the approach of adulthood comes a responsibility, shared by one's generation, not to allow worldly pursuits to blind one's eyes to injustice and privation. Over time, the qualities and attitudes nurtured by the courses of the training institute, through exposure to the Word of God, help individuals to see past the illusions that, at every stage of life, the world uses to pull attention away from service and towards the self. And ultimately, the systematic study of the Word of God and the exploration of its implications raises consciousness of the need to manage one's material affairs in keeping with the divine teachings.

Beloved Friends: The extremes of wealth and poverty in the world are becoming ever more untenable. As inequity persists, so the established order is seen to be unsure of itself, and its values are being questioned. Whatever the tribulations that a conflicted world must confront in the future, we pray that the Almighty will help His loved ones to overcome every obstacle in their path and assist them to serve humanity. The larger the presence of a Bahá'í community in a population, the greater its responsibility to find ways of addressing the root causes of the poverty in its surroundings. Although the friends are at the early stages of learning about such work and of contributing to the related discourses, the community-building process of the Five Year Plan is creating everywhere the ideal environment in which to accrue knowledge and experience, gradually but consistently, about the higher purpose of economic activity. Against the background of the age-long work of erecting a divine civilization, may this exploration become a more pronounced feature of community life, institutional thought, and individual action in the years ahead. (The Universal House of Justice, letter dated 1 March 2017, to the Bahá'ís of the World)

THE PROBLEM AND THE EFFECTS OF THE EXTREMES OF WEALTH AND POVERTY

The inordinate disparity between rich and poor, a source of acute suffering, keeps the world in a state of instability, virtually on the brink of war. Few societies have dealt effectively with this situation. The solution calls for the combined application of spiritual, moral and practical approaches. A fresh look at the problem is required, entailing consultation with experts from a wide spectrum of disciplines, devoid of economic and ideological polemics, and involving the people directly affected in the decisions that must urgently be made. It is an issue that is bound up not only with the necessity for eliminating extremes of wealth and poverty but also with those spiritual verities the understanding of which can produce a new universal attitude. Fostering such an attitude is itself a major part of the solution.
—The Universal House of Justice, *The Promise of World Peace,* ¶30

The Effects of Extreme Poverty Endanger All Humanity

The passionate and violent happenings that have, in recent years, strained to almost the point of complete breakdown the political and economic structure of society are too numerous and complex to attempt, within the limitations of this general survey, to arrive at an adequate estimate of their character. Nor have these tribulations, grievous as they have been, seemed to have reached their climax, and exerted the full force of their destructive power. The whole world, wherever and however we survey it, offers us the sad and pitiful spectacle of a vast, an enfeebled, and moribund organism, which is being torn politically and strangulated economically by forces it has ceased to either control or comprehend. (Shoghi Effendi, *The World Order of Bahá'u'lláh*, p. 188)

When such a crisis sweeps over the world no person should hope to remain intact. We belong to an organic unit and when one part of the organism suffers all the rest of the body will feel its consequence. This is in fact the reason why Bahá'u'lláh calls our attention to the unity of mankind. (From a letter written on behalf of Shoghi Effendi, dated 14 April 1932, to a Bahá'í family, in *Lights of Guidance*, no. 446)

With the fresh tide of political freedom resulting from the collapse of the strongholds of communism has come an explosion of nationalism. The concomitant rise of racism in many regions has become a matter of serious global concern. These are compounded by an upsurge in religious fundamentalism which is poisoning the wells of tolerance. Terrorism is rife. Widespread uncertainty about the condition of the economy indicates a deep disorder in the management of the material affairs of the planet, a condition which can only exacerbate the sense of frustration and futility affecting the political realm. The worsening state of the environment and of the health of huge populations is a source of alarm. (The Universal House of Justice, *A Wider Horizon, Selected Letters 1983–1992*, pp. 102–3)

The increasing disparity between the rich and the poor is a major destabilizing influence in the world. It produces or exacerbates regional and national conflicts, environmental degradation, crime and violence, and the increasing use of illicit drugs. These consequences of extreme poverty affect all individuals and nations. Increasingly we are becoming aware that we are all members of a single human family. In a family the suffering of any member is felt by all, and until that suffering is alleviated, no member of the family can be fully happy or at ease. Few are able to look at starvation and extreme poverty without feeling a sense of failure. (Bahá'í International Community,

February 12, 1993, Statement to the 49th Session of the United Nations
Commission on Human Rights, "Human Rights and Extreme Poverty")

The turmoil now convulsing human affairs is unprecedented, and many of
its consequences enormously destructive. Dangers unimagined in all history
gather around a distracted humanity. The greatest error that the world's leadership could make at this juncture, however, would be to allow the crisis to
cast doubt on the ultimate outcome of the process that is occurring. A world
is passing away and a new one is struggling to be born. The habits, attitudes,
and institutions that have accumulated over the centuries are being subjected
to tests that are as necessary to human development as they are inescapable.
What is required of the peoples of the world is a measure of faith and resolve
to match the enormous energies with which the Creator of all things has
endowed this spiritual springtime of the race. "Be united in counsel," is
Bahá'u'lláh's appeal, "be one in thought. May each morn be better than its
eve and each morrow richer than its yesterday. Man's merit lieth in service
and virtue and not in the pageantry of wealth and riches. Take heed that
your words be purged from idle fancies and worldly desires and your deeds
be cleansed from craftiness and suspicion. Dissipate not the wealth of your
precious lives in the pursuit of evil and corrupt affection, nor let your endeavors be spent in promoting your personal interest. Be generous in your days
of plenty, and be patient in the hour of loss. Adversity is followed by success
and rejoicings follow woe. Guard against idleness and sloth, and cling unto
that which profiteth mankind, whether young or old, whether high or low."
(Bahá'í International community, *The Prosperity of Humankind*)

The Lack of Unified Efforts for Resolving Societal Problems
Behold the disturbances which, for many a long year, have afflicted the earth,
and the perturbation that hath seized its peoples. It hath either been ravaged
by war, or tormented by sudden and unforeseen calamities. Though the
world is encompassed with misery and distress, yet no man hath paused to
reflect what the cause or source of that may be. Whenever the True Counsel-

lor uttered a word in admonishment, lo, they all denounced Him as a mover of mischief and rejected His claim. How bewildering, how confusing is such behavior! No two men can be found who may be said to be outwardly and inwardly united. The evidences of discord and malice are apparent everywhere, though all were made for harmony and union. (Bahá'u'lláh, *Tablets of Bahá'u'lláh*, pp. 163–64)

It is certain that the greatest of instrumentalities for achieving the advancement and the glory of man, the supreme agency for the enlightenment and the redemption of the world, is love and fellowship and unity among all the members of the human race. Nothing can be effected in the world, not even conceivably, without unity and agreement, and the perfect means for engendering fellowship and union is true religion. ('Abdu'l-Bahá, *The Secret of Divine Civilization*, ¶135)

As with the whole, so with the parts; whether a flower or a human body, when the attracting principle is withdrawn from it, the flower or the man dies. It is therefore clear that attraction, harmony, unity and love, are the cause of life, whereas repulsion, discord, hatred and separation bring death.

We have seen that whatever brings division into the world of existence causes death. ('Abdu'l-Bahá, *Paris Talks*, no. 42.7)

The whole of mankind is groaning, is dying to be led to unity, and to terminate its age-long martyrdom. And yet it stubbornly refuses to embrace the light and acknowledge the sovereign authority of the one Power that can extricate it from its entanglements, and avert the woeful calamity that threatens to engulf it. (Shoghi Effendi, *The World Order of Bahá'u'lláh*, p. 201)

Disunity is a danger that the nations and peoples of the earth can no longer endure; the consequences are too terrible to contemplate, too obvious to require any demonstration. (The Universal House of Justice, *The Promise of World Peace*, ¶54)

When Bahá'u'lláh proclaimed His Message to the world in the nineteenth century He made it abundantly clear that the first step essential for the peace and progress of mankind was its unification. As He says, "The well-being of mankind, its peace and security are unattainable unless and until its unity is firmly established." To this day, however, you will find most people take the opposite point of view: they look upon unity as an ultimate almost unattainable goal and concentrate first on remedying all the other ills of mankind. If they did but know it, these other ills are but various symptoms and side effects of the basic disease—disunity. (The Universal House of Justice, *Messages 1963 to 1986*, p. 125)

Disunity is the crux of the problems which so severely afflict the planet. It permeates attitudes in all departments of life. It is at the heart of all major conflicts between nations and peoples. More serious still, disunity is common in the relations between religions and within religions, vitiating the very spiritual and moral influence which it is their primary purpose to exert. "Should the lamp of religion be obscured," Bahá'u'lláh asserts, "chaos and confusion will ensue, and the lights of fairness, of justice, of tranquility and peace cease to shine." (The Universal House of Justice, 26 November 1992, Second Message to the World Congress)

Few will disagree that the universal disease sapping the health of the body of humankind is that of disunity. Its manifestations everywhere cripple political will, debilitate the collective urge to change, and poison national and religious relationships. How strange, then, that unity is regarded as a goal to be attained, if at all, in a distant future, after a host of disorders in social, political, economic and moral life have been addressed and somehow or other resolved. Yet the latter are essentially symptoms and side effects of the problem, not its root cause. Why has so fundamental an inversion of reality come to be widely accepted? The answer is presumably because the achievement of genuine unity of mind and heart among peoples whose experiences are deeply at variance is thought to be entirely beyond the capacity of society's existing institutions. While this tacit admission is a welcome advance over the understanding of processes of social evolution that prevailed a few decades ago, it is of limited practical assistance in responding to the challenge.

Unity is a condition of the human spirit. Education can support and enhance it, as can legislation, but they can do so only once it emerges and has established itself as a compelling force in social life. A global intelligentsia, its prescriptions largely shaped by materialistic misconceptions of reality, clings tenaciously to the hope that imaginative social engineering, supported by political compromise, may indefinitely postpone the potential disasters that few deny loom over humanity's future. "We can well perceive how the whole human race is encompassed with great, with incalculable afflictions," Bahá'u'lláh states. "They that are intoxicated by self-conceit have interposed themselves between it and the Divine and infallible Physician. Witness how they have entangled all men, themselves included, in the mesh of their devices. They can neither discover the cause of the disease, nor have they any knowledge of the remedy." As unity is the remedy for the world's ills, its one certain source lies in the restoration of religion's influence in human affairs. The laws and principles revealed by God, in this day, Bahá'u'lláh declares, "are the most potent instruments and the surest of all means for the dawning of the light of unity amongst men." (Prepared under the supervision of the Universal House of Justice, *One Common Faith*, pp. 42–43)

For unity to exist among human beings—at even the simplest level—two fundamental conditions must pertain. Those involved must first of all be in some agreement about the nature of reality as it affects their relationships with one another and with the phenomenal world. They must, secondly, give assent to some recognized and authoritative means by which decisions will be taken that affect their association with one another and that determine their collective goals.

Unity is not, that is, merely a condition resulting from a sense of mutual goodwill and common purpose, however profound and sincerely held such sentiments may be, any more than an organism is a product of some fortuitous and amorphous association of various elements. Unity is a phenomenon of creative power, whose existence becomes apparent through the effects that collective action produces and whose absence is betrayed by the impotence of such efforts. However handicapped it often has been by ignorance and perversity, this force has been the primary influence driving the advancement of civilization, generating legal codes, social and political institutions, artistic works, technological achievements without end, moral breakthroughs, material prosperity, and long periods of public peace whose afterglow lived in the memories of subsequent generations as imagined "golden ages." (Prepared under the supervision of the Universal House of Justice, *Century of Light,* p. 40)

It is important, at the outset, to acknowledge that poverty is a condition that arises from the injustices of society. The very structures that perpetuate poverty also perpetuate the lack of participation of the materially poor in decisions that affect their lives. Too often, those living in poverty are not treated as part of society; social norms and structures, legal mechanisms and economic policies develop in ways that, either explicitly or not, exclude them from full participation. Despite noble intentions, many efforts to remedy the situation place the burden of responsibility on the very populations struggling within systems that deny them access to channels of deliberation and decision-making. Yet the responsibility lies with society—its communities and social institutions—to make it possible for all people to contribute their energies and talents to the construction of a more just and equitable global community. . . .

A key question, then, is whether efforts to involve the materially poor in decision-making conceive of their contribution as being relevant for the well-being of society as whole, or whether their involvement is understood merely within the context of projects created by others—generally those with access to resources and power. The question is an important one, for if involvement is limited to processes designed and built by others, it must be understood that such "participation," by giving implicit consent to the process, runs the risk of reinforcing the structures that perpetuate inequities. As one prominent thinker has noted, authentic development occurs when groups become the subjects who deliberate, decide and act in the world, rather than being either victims of circumstance or objects of someone else's decisions.

It is an unfortunate reality that participatory mechanisms designed for those living in poverty often take the form of *pro forma* consultations or largely symbolic "listening-sessions." Such approaches demonstrate that involvement, by itself, is no panacea, and that consensus can as easily be the product of manipulation by those with vested interests, as the product of authentic participation. Participation must therefore be substantive and creative if it is to further constructive social transformation. It must engage constituents in the full range of the decision-making process, from identifying challenges, devising solutions, choosing approaches to determining implementation strategies and articulating criteria for evaluation. In particular, the more individuals are included in the early stages of the process, the more fully they can express their agency.

Creating an environment in which all people, particularly the historically excluded and marginalized, are able to take part in decision-making processes also requires a transformation at the level of the individual. The present-day social order, in which materialism and exploitation have largely supplanted the organizing principles of justice and mutualism, exerts its influence on each one of us and shapes our understanding of ourselves and our role in society. The exclusion of individuals from relevant decision-making processes, the failure of society to consider their needs and aspirations, too often distorts their perceptions of their dignity and self-worth. Expanding meaningful opportunities for participation, then, has intrinsic value as it respects the inherent worth and dignity of marginalized peoples and provides an environment in which their experiences, perspectives, their hopes and fears can be heard.

Expanding the participation of those who have historically been excluded from decision-making not only increases the pool of intellectual resources, but can also foster the trust and mutual commitment needed for sustained, collective action. A diversity of opinions, on its own, however, does not provide a means to bridge differences or resolve social tensions. A unifying process of decision-making is needed—one which helps participants to formulate common goals, to manage collective resources, to win the good-will and support of all stakeholders, and to mobilize diverse talents and capacities. . . .

Reaching a shared vision of action requires processes of collective inquiry and decision-making that focus on ascertaining facts and assessing circumstances, rather than on advancing competing claims and interests. In such an atmosphere, ideas that have been shared no longer "belong" to the individuals who expressed them, but become a resource to be adopted, modified or discarded by the group as a whole. And while individuals are free to express differing opinions and viewpoints in a candid and frank manner, interactions need to be dignified and guided by a shared search for the truth about a given situation. (Bahá'í International Community, 14 December 2012, "Towards Full and Meaningful Participation of Persons Living in Poverty in Shaping Processes and Structures That Impact Their Lives")

What Bahá'u'lláh is calling for is a consultative process in which the individual participants strive to transcend their respective points of view, in order to function as members of a body with its own interests and goals. In such an atmosphere, characterized by both candor and courtesy, ideas belong not to the individual to whom they occur during the discussion but to the group as a whole, to take up, discard, or revise as seems to best serve the goal pursued. Consultation succeeds to the extent that all participants support the decisions arrived at, regardless of the individual opinions with which they entered the discussion. Under such circumstances an earlier decision can be readily reconsidered if experience exposes any shortcomings.

Viewed in such a light, consultation is the operating expression of justice in human affairs. (Bahá'í International Community, *The Prosperity of Humankind*)

Injustice, Tyranny, and Oppression

Justice is, in this day, bewailing its plight, and Equity groaneth beneath the yoke of oppression. The thick clouds of tyranny have darkened the face of the earth, and enveloped its peoples. (Bahá'u'lláh, *Gleanings from the Writings of Bahá'u'lláh*, no. 63.2)

In these days truthfulness and sincerity are sorely afflicted in the clutches of falsehood, and justice is tormented by the scourge of injustice. The smoke of corruption hath enveloped the whole world in such wise that naught can be seen in any direction save regiments of soldiers and nothing is heard from any land but the clashing of swords. We beseech God, the True One, to strengthen the wielders of His power in that which will rehabilitate the world and bring tranquility to the nations. (Bahá'u'lláh, *Tablets of Bahá'u'lláh*, p. 39)

The light of Justice is dimmed, and the sun of Equity veiled from sight. The robber occupieth the seat of the protector and guard, and the position of the faithful is seized by the traitor. . . . In the abundance of Our grace and loving-kindness We have revealed specially for the rulers and ministers of the world that which is conducive to safety and protection, tranquility and peace; haply the children of men may rest secure from the evils of oppression. He, verily, is the Protector, the Helper, the Giver of victory. (Bahá'u'lláh, *Tablets of Bahá'u'lláh*, p. 124)

And among the teachings of Bahá'u'lláh are justice and right. Until these are realized on the plane of existence, all things shall be in disorder and remain imperfect. The world of mankind is a world of oppression and cruelty, and a realm of aggression and error. ('Abdu'l-Bahá, *Selections from the Writings of 'Abdu'l-Bahá*, no. 227.24)

With respect to social issues, . . . grave problems persist. While new levels of consensus have been reached on global programs to promote health, sustainable development and human rights, the situation on the ground in many areas has deteriorated. The alarming spread of militant racialism and religious fanaticism, the cancerous growth of materialism, the epidemic rise of crime and organized criminality, the widespread increase in mindless violence, the ever-deepening disparity between rich and poor, the continuing inequities faced by women, the intergenerational damage caused by the pervasive breakdown of family life, the immoral excesses of unbridled capitalism and the growth of political corruption—all speak to this point. At least a billion live in abject poverty and more than a third of the world's people are illiterate. (Bahá'í International Community, October 1995, *Turning Point For All Nations*)

Inadequate Legislation for Social Justice
Today no state in the world is in a condition of peace or tranquility, for security and trust have vanished from among the people. Both the governed and the governors are alike in danger. ('Abdu'l-Bahá, *Selections from the Writings of 'Abdu'l-Bahá*, no. 225.27)

It is evident that under present systems and conditions of government the poor are subject to the greatest need and distress while others more fortunate live in luxury and plenty far beyond their actual necessities. This inequality of portion and privilege is one of the deep and vital problems of human society. That there is need of an equalization and apportionment by which all may possess the comforts and privileges of life is evident. The remedy must be legislative readjustment of conditions. The rich too must be merciful to the poor, contributing from willing hearts to their needs without being forced or compelled to do so. The composure of the world will be assured by

19

the establishment of this principle in the religious life of mankind. ('Abdu'l-Bahá, *The Promulgation of Universal Peace*, p. 148)

There must be special laws made, dealing with these extremes of riches and of want. The members of the Government should consider the laws of God when they are framing plans for the ruling of the people. The general rights of mankind must be guarded and preserved.

The government of the countries should conform to the Divine Law which gives equal justice to all. This is the only way in which the deplorable superfluity of great wealth and miserable, demoralizing, degrading poverty can be abolished. Not until this is done will the Law of God be obeyed. ('Abdu'l-Bahá, *Paris Talks*, no. 46.12–13)

Racism Blights Human Progress

And the breeding-ground of all these tragedies is prejudice: prejudice of race and nation, of religion, of political opinion; and the root cause of prejudice is blind imitation of the past—imitation in religion, in racial attitudes, in national bias, in politics. So long as this aping of the past persisteth, just so long will the foundations of the social order be blown to the four winds, just so long will humanity be continually exposed to direst peril. ('Abdu'l-Bahá, *Selections from the Writings of 'Abdu'l-Bahá*, no. 202.3)

Again, as to religious, racial, national and political bias: all these prejudices strike at the very root of human life; one and all they beget bloodshed, and the ruination of the world. So long as these prejudices survive, there will be continuous and fearsome wars. ('Abdu'l-Bahá, *Selections from the Writings of 'Abdu'l-Bahá*, no. 202.10)

Bahá'u'lláh also taught that prejudices—whether religious, racial, patriotic or political—are destructive to the foundations of human development. Prejudices of any kind are the destroyers of human happiness and welfare.

Until they are dispelled, the advancement of the world of humanity is not possible; yet racial, religious and national biases are observed everywhere. For thousands of years the world of humanity has been agitated and disturbed by prejudices. As long as it prevails, warfare, animosity and hatred will continue. Therefore, if we seek to establish peace, we must cast aside this obstacle; for otherwise, agreement and composure are not to be attained. ('Abdu'l-Bahá, *The Promulgation of Universal Peace*, p. 252)

Racism, one of the most baneful and persistent evils, is a major barrier to peace. Its practice perpetrates too outrageous a violation of the dignity of human beings to be countenanced under any pretext. Racism retards the unfoldment of the boundless potentialities of its victims, corrupts its perpetrators, and blights human progress. Recognition of the oneness of mankind, implemented by appropriate legal measures, must be universally upheld if this problem is to be overcome. (The Universal House of Justice, *The Promise of World Peace*, ¶29)

Many of your questions relate to the relative seriousness of the race issue as compared to other issues. You ask, for example, whether the building of harmony between the races is still "the most vital and challenging issue facing the American Bahá'í community." What is more important to understand is that the achievement of race unity is far from complete. There is little to be gained by trying to invent a precise way of ranking various complex problems such as racism or by attempting to resolve these problems on a piecemeal basis. The piecemeal efforts of those outside of the Bahá'í community who are concerned with the many grievous ills facing humanity have had little lasting success. Their well-meaning endeavours have suffered from a lack of appreciation of the spiritual origin of these illnesses and a lack of understanding that the only lasting solution lies in acceptance of the remedies of the Divine Physician. (From a letter written on behalf of the Universal House of Justice, dated 24 March 1998, to an individual)

From the Bahá'í perspective, racism is tenacious because it is not confined to its more apparent manifestations of political oppression and strife, . . . or economic inequality and exploitation. Rather, racism is enduring because it first takes root in the minds and consciences of individuals. It involves learned behavior, the expression of racial prejudice in individual hearts. (Bahá'í International Community, "Combating Racism")

Just as a fever is a symptom of disease in the body, racism is a symptom of disease in society. Suppressing the symptom does not cure the disease, but curing the disease eliminates the symptom. The Bahá'í International Community is convinced that the disease from which society currently suffers is failure to recognize the principle of the oneness of humanity, and racism is but a symptom. If we wish to eliminate racism entirely, we must establish, as the moral of foundation for society, the unshakable conviction of the oneness of the human race. (Bahá'í International Community, "Eliminating Racism")

The Lack of Human Kindness and Cooperation
Every human being has the right to live; they have a right to rest, and to a certain amount of well-being. As a rich man is able to live in his palace surrounded by luxury and the greatest comfort, so should a poor man be able to have the necessaries of life. Nobody should die of hunger; everybody should have sufficient clothing; one man should not live in excess while another has no possible means of existence.

Let us try with all the strength we have to bring about happier conditions, so that no single soul may be destitute. ('Abdu'l-Bahá, *Paris Talks,* no. 40.23–24)

. . . that some are happy and comfortable and some in misery, some are accumulating exorbitant wealth and others are in dire want—under such a system it is impossible for man to be happy and impossible for him to win the good pleasure of God. God is kind to all. The good pleasure of God consists in the welfare of all the individual members of mankind.

A Persian king was one night in his palace, living in the greatest luxury and comfort. Through excessive joy and gladness he addressed a certain man, saying, "Of all my life this is the happiest moment. Praise be to God, from every point prosperity appears and fortune smiles! My treasury is full and the army is well taken care of. My palaces are many; my land unlimited; my family is well off; my honor and sovereignty are great. What more could I want?"

The poor man at the gate of his palace spoke out, saying: "O kind king! Assuming that you are from every point of view so happy, free from every worry and sadness, do you not worry for us? You say that on your own account you have no worries, but do you never worry about the poor in your land? Is it becoming or meet that you should be so well off and we in such dire want and need? In view of our needs and troubles, how can you rest in your palace, how can you even say that you are free from worries and sorrows? As a ruler you must not be so egoistic as to think of yourself alone, but you must think of those who are your subjects. When we are comfortable, then you will be comfortable; when we are in misery, how can you, as a king, be in happiness?"

The purport is this, that we are all inhabiting one globe of earth. In reality we are one family, and each one of us is a member of this family. We must all be in the greatest happiness and comfort, under a just rule and regulation which is according to the good pleasure of God, thus causing us to be happy, for this life is fleeting.

If man were to care for himself only he would be nothing but an animal, for only the animals are thus egoistic. If you bring a thousand sheep to a well to kill nine hundred and ninety-nine, the one remaining sheep would go on grazing, not thinking of the others and worrying not at all about the lost, never bothering that its own kind had passed away, or had perished or been killed. To look after one's self only is, therefore, an animal propensity. It is the animal propensity to live solitary and alone. It is the animal proclivity to look after one's own comfort. But man was created to be a man—to be fair, to be just, to be merciful, to be kind to all his species, never to be willing that he himself be well off while others are in misery and distress. This is an attribute of the animal and not of man. Nay, rather, man should be willing to accept hardships for himself in order that others may enjoy wealth; he should enjoy trouble for himself that others may enjoy happiness and well-being. This is the attribute of man. This is becoming of man. Otherwise man is not man—he is less than the animal.

The man who thinks only of himself and is thoughtless of others is undoubtedly inferior to the animal because the animal is not possessed of the reasoning faculty. The animal is excused; but in man there is reason, the faculty of justice, the faculty of mercifulness. Possessing all these faculties, he must not leave them unused. He who is so hard-hearted as to think only of his own comfort, such an one will not be called man. ('Abdu'l-Bahá, *The Promulgation of Universal Peace*, pp. 440–41)

It seems as though all creatures can exist singly and alone. For example, a tree can exist solitary and alone on a given prairie or in a valley or on the mountainside. An animal upon a mountain or a bird soaring in the air might live a solitary life. They are not in need of cooperation or solidarity. Such animated beings enjoy the greatest comfort and happiness in their respective solitary lives.

On the contrary, man cannot live singly and alone. He is in need of continuous cooperation and mutual help. For example, a man living alone in the wilderness will eventually starve. He can never, singly and alone, provide himself with all the necessities of existence. Therefore, he is in need of cooperation and reciprocity. The mystery of this phenomenon, the cause thereof is this: that mankind has been created from one single origin, has branched off from one family. Thus, in reality, all mankind represents one family. God has not created any difference. He has created all as one that thus this family might live in perfect happiness and well-being.

Regarding reciprocity and cooperation, each member of the body politic should live in the utmost comfort and welfare because each individual member of humanity is a member of the body politic, and if one member is in distress or is afflicted with some disease, all the other members must necessarily suffer. For example, a member of the human organism is the eye. If the eye should be affected, that affliction would affect the whole nervous system. Hence, if a member of the body politic becomes afflicted, in reality, from the standpoint of sympathetic connection, all will share that affliction since this [one afflicted] is a member of the group of members, a part of the whole. Is it possible for one member or part to be in distress and the other members to be at ease? It is impossible! Hence, God has desired that in the body politic of humanity each one shall enjoy perfect welfare and comfort.

Although the body politic is one family, yet, because of lack of harmonious relations some members are comfortable and some in direst misery; some members are satisfied and some are hungry; some members are clothed in most costly garments and some families are in need of food and shelter. Why? Because this family lacks the necessary reciprocity and symmetry. This household is not well arranged. This household is not living under a perfect law. All the laws which are legislated do not ensure happiness. They do not provide comfort. Therefore, a law must be given to this family by means of which all the members of this family will enjoy equal well-being and happiness.

Is it possible for one member of a family to be subjected to the utmost misery and to abject poverty and for the rest of the family to be comfortable? It is impossible unless those members of the family be senseless, atrophied, inhospitable, unkind. Then they would say, "Though these members do belong to our family, let them alone. Let us look after ourselves. Let them die. So long as I am comfortable, I am honored, I am happy—this, my brother—let him die. If he be in misery, let him remain in misery, so long as I am comfortable. If he is hungry, let him remain so; I am satisfied. If he is without clothes, so long as I am clothed, let him remain as he is. If he is shelterless, homeless, so long as I have a home, let him remain in the wilderness."

Such utter indifference in the human family is due to lack of control, to lack of a working law, to lack of kindness in its midst. If kindness had been shown to the members of this family, surely all the members thereof would have enjoyed comfort and happiness. ('Abdu'l-Bahá, *The Promulgation of Universal Peace*, pp. 435–37)

Materialism, Immorality, and Absence of Spiritual Values

Observe how darkness has overspread the world. In every corner of the earth there is strife, discord and warfare of some kind. Mankind is submerged in the sea of materialism and occupied with the affairs of this world. They have no thought beyond earthly possessions and manifest no desire save the passions of this fleeting, mortal existence. Their utmost purpose is the attainment of material livelihood, physical comforts and worldly enjoyments such as constitute the happiness of the animal world rather than the world of man. ('Abdu'l-Bahá, *The Promulgation of Universal Peace*, p. 474)

No matter how far the material world advances, it cannot establish the happiness of mankind. Only when material and spiritual civilization are linked and coordinated will happiness be assured. Then material civilization will not contribute its energies to the forces of evil in destroying the oneness of humanity, for in material civilization good and evil advance together and maintain the same pace. For example, consider the material progress of man in the last decade. Schools and colleges, hospitals, philanthropic institutions, scientific academies and temples of philosophy have been founded, but hand in hand with these evidences of development, the invention and production of means and weapons for human destruction have correspondingly increased. In early days the weapon of war was the sword; now it is the magazine rifle. Among the ancients, men fought with javelins and daggers; now they employ shells and bombs. Dreadnoughts are built, torpedoes invented, and every few days new ammunition is forthcoming.

All this is the outcome of material civilization; therefore, although material advancement furthers good purposes in life, at the same time it serves evil

26

ends. The divine civilization is good because it cultivates morals. ('Abdu'l-Bahá, *The Promulgation of Universal Peace*, p. 151)

East and West have joined to worship stars of faded splendor and have turned in prayer unto darkened horizons.

Both have utterly neglected the broad foundation of God's sacred laws, and have grown unmindful of the merits and virtues of His religion.

They have regarded certain customs and conventions as the immutable basis of the Divine Faith, and have firmly established themselves therein. They have imagined themselves as having attained the glorious pinnacle of achievement and prosperity when, in reality, they have touched the innermost depths of heedlessness and deprived themselves wholly of God's bountiful gifts.

The cornerstone of the Religion of God is the acquisition of the Divine perfections and the sharing in His manifold bestowals. The essential purpose of faith and belief is to ennoble the inner being of man with the outpourings of grace from on high. If this be not attained, it is indeed deprivation itself. It is the torment of infernal fire. ('Abdu'l-Bahá, in *Bahá'í World*, vol. 11, p. 658)

. . . their ideologies, are to be commonly condemned by the upholders of the standard of the Faith of Bahá'u'lláh for their materialistic philosophies and their neglect of those spiritual values and eternal verities on which alone a stable and flourishing civilization can be ultimately established. (Shoghi Effendi, *Citadel of Faith*, p. 125)

Indeed the chief reason for the evils now rampant in society is the lack of spirituality. The materialistic civilization of our age has so much absorbed the energy and interest of mankind that people in general do no longer feel the necessity of raising themselves above the forces and conditions of their daily material existence. There is not sufficient demand for things that we call spiritual to differentiate them from the needs and requirements of our physical existence.

The universal crisis affecting mankind is, therefore, essentially spiritual in its causes. The spirit of the age, taken on the whole, is irreligious. Man's outlook on life is too crude and materialistic to enable him to elevate himself into the higher realms of the spirit. (Shoghi Effendi, *Directives from the Guardian,* p. 86)

Collateral with this ominous laxity in morals, and this progressive stress laid on man's material pursuits and well-being, is the darkening of the political horizon, as witnessed by the widening of the gulf separating the protagonists of two antagonistic schools of thought which, however divergent in the condition that the world is in is bringing many issues to a head. It would be perhaps impossible to find a nation or people not in a state of crisis today. The materialism, the lack of true religion and the consequent baser forces in human nature which are being released, have brought the whole world to the brink of probably the greatest crisis it has ever faced or will have to face. (From a letter written on behalf of Shoghi Effendi, dated 19 July 1956, to the National Spiritual Assembly of the United States, in *Lights of Guidance,* no. 440)

Our troubles are not purely economic. There are also basic spiritual reforms that have to set in. There is the human heart that has to be changed.

We cannot segregate the human heart from the environment outside us and say that once one of these is reformed everything will be improved. Man is organic with the world. His inner life moulds the environment and is itself also deeply affected by it. The one acts upon the other and every abiding change in the life of man is the result of these mutual reactions. (From a letter written on behalf of Shoghi Effendi, dated 17 February 1933, to an individual, in *Social and Economic Development,* p. 8)

You had asked about poverty and wealth, and the toil of the poor and the comfort of the rich, and you had expressed your amazement and wonder at this situation. . . .

THE PROBLEM AND THE EFFECTS OF THE EXTREMES
OF WEALTH AND POVERTY

It is evident that the subject of the suffering poor and the pampered rich has been, and will continue to be, discussed by the world's scholars and philosophers, but so far they have not found a solution to this difficult problem. Whatever you witness in this world, such as evidences of mighty upheavals and omens of future events, all revolve around this pivot, that is, the groaning and the agitation of the poor on the one hand, and the excessive wealth and affluence of the rich on the other. This conflict and clash of interests will remain unchanged until such time as the laws and commandments revealed by the Pen of the Most High in this regard are executed and enforced, and the solution of the economic problems based on spiritual principles becomes possible. Then will there be peace between the rich and the poor, or between the forces of capital and labour. Then will the poor gain their legitimate right of having their necessary and essential needs satisfied, and the rich will be able to spend their wealth as they please, free of fear for their lives and property. The intent is not, however, to say that all the poor will become rich and they will become equal. Such a concept is like saying that all the ignorant and the illiterate will become the sages of the age and the learned of the learned. Rather, when education becomes compulsory and universal, ignorance and illiteracy will decrease and there will remain no one deprived of education. But, as the basis for distinction is in the person's capacity and ability, and differences are related to the degree of his intelligence and mental powers, therefore, all the people will not be equal in their knowledge, learning and understanding. The intent is to say that the world of creation calls for distinctions in people's stations, and degrees in the differences existing among them, so that the affairs of the world may become organized and ordered. Diversity in all created things, whether in kind, in physical appearance, or in station, is the means for their protection, their permanence, unity and harmony. Each part complements the other.

Concerning the point that the poor are always in hardship and trouble and in need of everything, this we can acknowledge. However, it is doubtful whether the rich have peace of mind and true comfort, they should be quietly asked about this, and their response is dependent upon their conscience.

(From a letter written on behalf of Shoghi Effendi, dated 22 May 1928, in
"Economics, Agriculture, and Related Subjects," pp. 7–8)

In the wake of such horrendous disruptions, there have been unexampled
advances in the realms of science, technology and social organization; a veritable explosion of knowledge; and an even more remarkable burgeoning in
the awakening and rise of masses of humanity which were previously presumed to be dormant. These masses are claiming their rightful places within
the community of nations which has greatly expanded. With the simultane-
ous development of communications at the speed of light and transportation
at the speed of sound, the world has contracted into a mere neighborhood in
which people are instantly aware of each other's affairs and have immediate
access to each other. And yet, even with such miraculous advances, with
the emergence of international organizations, and with valiant attempts and
brilliant successes at international cooperation, nations are at woeful odds
with one another, people are convulsed by economic upheavals, races feel
more alienated than before and are filled with mistrust, humiliation and fear.

Collateral with these changes has been the breakdown of institutions,
religious and political, which traditionally functioned as the guideposts for
the stability of society. Even the most resilient of these seem to be losing
their credibility as they have become preoccupied with their own internal
disorder. This calls attention to the emptiness of the moral landscape and the
feeling of futility deranging personal life. Thoughtful commentators write
apprehensively about the fall of culture and the consequent disappearance
of values, the loss of the fullness of the inner life, a technological civilization
facing an increasingly serious crisis. They write, moreover, of the human
species as being at the end with its wisdom and being unable to control itself,
of the need for divine wisdom and foresight, and of the human psyche as
being far removed from recognizing this need.

These ominous comments reflect the universal consequences of a failed
understanding as to the purpose of God for humankind. It is in this particular respect that the Revelation of Bahá'u'lláh sheds new light; it refreshes our

30

thoughts; it clarifies and expands our conceptions. His Teachings imbue us with the abundance of God's love for His creatures; they impress upon us the indispensability of justice in human relations and emphasize the importance of adhering to principle in all matters; they inform us that human beings have been created "to carry forward an ever-advancing civilization" and that the virtues that befit the dignity of every person are: "forbearance, mercy, compassion and loving-kindness towards all the peoples and kindreds of the earth." (The Universal House of Justice, dated 26 November 1992, Second Message to World Congress, pp. 1–2)

The time has come when those who preach the dogmas of materialism, whether of the east or the west, whether of capitalism or socialism, must give account of the moral stewardship they have presumed to exercise. Where is the "new world" promised by these ideologies? Where is the international peace to whose ideals they proclaim their devotion? Where are the breakthroughs into new realms of cultural achievement produced by the aggrandizement of this race, of that nation or of a particular class? Why is the vast majority of the world's peoples sinking ever deeper into hunger and wretchedness when wealth on a scale undreamed of by the Pharaohs, the Caesars, or even the imperialist powers of the nineteenth century is at the disposal of the present arbiters of human affairs?

Most particularly, it is in the glorification of material pursuits, at once the progenitor and common feature of all such ideologies, that we find the roots which nourish the falsehood that human beings are incorrigibly selfish and aggressive. It is here that the ground must be cleared for the building of a new world fit for our descendants.

That materialistic ideals have, in the light of experience, failed to satisfy the needs of mankind calls for an honest acknowledgement that a fresh effort must now be made to find the solutions to the agonizing problems of the planet. The intolerable conditions pervading society bespeak a common failure of all, a circumstance which tends to incite rather than relieve the entrenchment on every side. Clearly, a common remedial effort is urgently required. It is primarily a matter of attitude. Will humanity continue in its waywardness, holding to outworn concepts and unworkable assumptions? Or will its leaders, regardless of ideology, step forth and, with a resolute will, consult together in a united search for appropriate solutions? (The Universal House of Justice, *The Promise of World Peace,* ¶21–23)

. . . we must not allow ourselves to forget the continuing, appalling burden of suffering under which millions of human beings are always groaning—a burden which they have borne for century upon century and which it is the Mission of Bahá'u'lláh to lift at last. The principal cause of this suffering, which one can witness wherever one turns, is the corruption of human morals and the prevalence of prejudice, suspicion, hatred, untrustworthiness, selfishness and tyranny among men. It is not merely material well-being that people need. What they desperately need is to know how to live their lives—they need to know who they are, to what purpose they exist, and how they should act towards one another; and, once they know the answers to these questions they need to be helped to gradually apply these answers to every-day behavior. It is to the solution of this basic problem of mankind that the greater part of all our energy and resources should be directed. (From a letter written on behalf of the Universal House of Justice, dated 19 November 1974, to the National Spiritual Assembly of Italy, in *Messages 1963 to 1986,* no. 151.5)

Every discerning eye clearly sees that the early stages of this chaos have daily manifestations affecting the structure of human society; its destructive forces are uprooting time-honored institutions which were a haven and refuge for the inhabitants of the earth in bygone days and centuries, and around which revolved all human affairs. The same destructive forces are also deranging the political, economic, scientific, literary, and moral equilibrium of the world and are destroying the fairest fruits of the present civilization. Political machinations of those in authority have placed the seal of obsolescence upon the root principles of the world's order. Greed and passion, deceit, hypocrisy, tyranny, and pride are dominating features afflicting human relations. Discoveries and inventions, which are the fruit of scientific and technological advancements, have become the means and tools of mass extermination and destruction and are in the hands of the ungodly. Even music, art, and literature, which are to represent and inspire the noblest sentiments and highest aspirations and should be a source of comfort and tranquility for troubled souls, have strayed from the straight path and are now the mirrors of the soiled hearts of this confused, unprincipled, and disordered age. Perversions such as these shall result in the ordeals which have been prophesied by the Blessed Beauty in the following words: ". . . the earth will be tormented by a fresh calamity every day and unprecedented commotions will break out." "The day is approaching when its [civilization's] flame will devour the cities." (From a letter written on behalf of the Universal House of Justice, dated 10 February 1980, to the Iranian believers resident in various countries throughout the world, in *Messages 1963 to 1986,* no. 246.4)

All over the world tremendous efforts are being made to improve the lot of mankind—or of parts of mankind, but most of these efforts are frustrated by conflicts of aims, by corruption of the morals of those involved, by mistrust, or by fear. There is no lack of material resources in the world if they are properly used. The problem is the education of human beings in the ultimate and most important purpose of life and in how to weld differences of opinion and outlook into a united constructive effort. Bahá'ís believe that God has revealed the purpose of life, has shown us how to attain it, has provided the ways in which we can work together and, beyond that, has given mankind the assurance both of continuing divine guidance and of divine assistance. As people learn and follow these teachings their efforts will produce durable results. In the absence of these teachings, a lifetime of effort only too often ends in disillusionment and the collapse of all that has been built. (From a letter written on behalf of the Universal House of Justice, dated 3 January 1982, to an individual believer, in *Messages 1963 to 1986,* no. 308.11)

Tragically, what Bahá'ís see in present-day society is unbridled exploitation of the masses of humanity by greed that excuses itself as the operation of "impersonal market forces." What meets their eyes everywhere is the destruction of moral foundations vital to humanity's future, through gross self-indulgence masquerading as "freedom of speech." What they find themselves struggling against daily is the pressure of a dogmatic materialism, claiming to be the voice of "science," that seeks systematically to exclude from intellectual life all impulses arising from the spiritual level of human consciousness. (Prepared under the supervision of the Universal House of Justice, *Century of Light*, p. 136)

. . . it is no longer possible to maintain the belief that the approach to social and economic development to which the materialistic conception of life has given rise is capable of meeting humanity's needs. Optimistic forecasts about the changes it would generate have vanished into the ever-widening abyss that separates the living standards of a small and relatively diminishing minority of the world's inhabitants from the poverty experienced by the vast majority of the globe's population.

This unprecedented economic crisis, together with the social breakdown it has helped to engender, reflects a profound error of conception about human nature itself. For the levels of response elicited from human beings by the incentives of the prevailing order are not only inadequate, but seem almost irrelevant in the face of world events. We are being shown that, unless the development of society finds a purpose beyond the mere amelioration of material conditions, it will fail of attaining even these goals. That purpose must be sought in spiritual dimensions of life and motivation that transcend a constantly changing economic landscape. . . . (Bahá'í International Community, *The Prosperity of Humankind*)

Inadequate Education

Close investigation will show that the primary cause of oppression and injustice, of unrighteousness, irregularity and disorder, is the people's lack of religious faith and the fact that they are uneducated. When, for example, the people are genuinely religious and are literate and well-schooled, and a difficulty presents itself, they can apply to the local authorities; if they do not meet with justice and secure their rights and if they see that the conduct of the local government is incompatible with the Divine good pleasure and the king's justice, they can then take their case to higher courts and describe the deviation of the local administration from the spiritual law. Those courts can then send for the local records of the case and in this way justice will be done. At present, however, because of their inadequate schooling, most of the population lack even the vocabulary to explain what they want. ('Abdu'l-Bahá, *The Secret of Divine Civilization*, ¶34)

The cause of universal education, which has already enlisted in its service an army of dedicated people from every faith and nation, deserves the utmost support that the governments of the world can lend it. For ignorance is indisputably the principle reason for the decline and fall of people and the perpetuation of prejudice. No nation can achieve success unless education is accorded all its citizens. Lack of resources limits the ability of many nations to fulfil this necessity, imposing a certain ordering of priorities. (The Universal House of Justice, *The Promise of World Peace*, ¶34)

Moreover, as the experience of recent decades has demonstrated, material benefits and endeavors cannot be regarded as ends in themselves. Their value consists not only in providing for humanity's basic needs in housing, food, health care, and the like, but in extending the reach of human abilities. The most important role that economic efforts must play in development lies, therefore, in equipping people and institutions with the means through which they can achieve the real purpose of development: that is, laying foundations for a new social order that can cultivate the limitless potentialities latent in human consciousness.

Only in this way can economics and the related sciences free themselves from the undertow of the materialistic preoccupations that now distract them, and fulfil their potential as tools vital to achieving human well-being in the full sense of the term. Nowhere is the need for a rigorous dialogue between the work of science and the insights of religion more apparent. (Bahá'í International Community, 16 July 1995, "The Realization of Economic, Social and Cultural Rights")

Universal education will be an indispensable contributor to this process of capacity building, but the effort will succeed only as human affairs are so reorganized as to enable both individuals and groups in every sector of society to acquire knowledge and apply it to the shaping of human affairs. (Bahá'í International Community, *The Prosperity of Humankind*)

The Failure of World Leaders to Adjust National Policies to the Needs of an Interdependent World

"The Tongue of Grandeur," Bahá'u'lláh Himself affirms, "hath . . . in the Day of His Manifestation proclaimed: 'It is not his to boast who loveth his country, but it is his who loveth the world.'" "Through the power," He adds, "released by these exalted words He hath lent a fresh impulse, and set a new direction, to the birds of men's hearts, and hath obliterated every trace of restriction and limitation from God's Holy Book."

A word of warning should, however, be uttered in this connection. The love of one's country, instilled and stressed by the teaching of Islam, as "an element of the Faith of God," has not, through this declaration, this clarion-call of Bahá'u'lláh, been either condemned or disparaged. It should not, indeed it cannot, be construed as a repudiation, or regarded in the light of a censure, pronounced against a sane and intelligent patriotism, nor does it seek to undermine the allegiance and loyalty of any individual to his country, nor does it conflict with the legitimate aspirations, rights, and duties of any individual state or nation. All it does imply and proclaim is the insufficiency of patriotism, in view of the fundamental changes effected in the economic life of society and the interdependence of the nations, and as the consequence of the contraction of the world, through the revolution in the means of transportation and communication—conditions that did not and could not exist either in the days of Jesus Christ or of Muhammad. It calls for a wider loyalty, which should not, and indeed does not, conflict with lesser loyalties. It instills a love which, in view of its scope, must include and not exclude the love of one's own country. It lays, through this loyalty which it inspires, and this love which it infuses, the only foundation on which the concept of world citizenship can thrive, and the structure of world unification can rest. It does insist, however, on the subordination of national considerations and particularistic interests to the imperative and paramount claims of humanity as a whole, inasmuch as in a world of interdependent nations and peoples the advantage of the part is best to be reached by the advantage of the whole. (Shoghi Effendi, *The Promised Day is Come*, ¶298–99)

Is it not a fact—and this is the central idea I desire to emphasize—that the fundamental cause of this world unrest is attributable, . . . to the failure of those into whose hands the immediate destinies of peoples and nations have been committed, to adjust their system of economic and political institutions to the imperative needs of a rapidly evolving age? Are not these intermittent crises that convulse present-day society due primarily to the lamentable inability of the world's recognized leaders to read aright the signs of the times, to rid themselves once for all of their preconceived ideas and fettering creeds, and to reshape the machinery of their respective governments according to those standards that are implicit in Bahá'u'lláh's supreme declaration of the Oneness of Mankind—the chief and distinguishing feature of the Faith He proclaimed? For the principle of the Oneness of Mankind, the cornerstone of Bahá'u'lláh's world-embracing dominion, implies nothing more nor less than the enforcement of His scheme for the unification of the world—the scheme to which we have already referred. "In every Dispensation," writes 'Abdu'l-Bahá, "the light of Divine Guidance has been focused upon one central theme. . . . In this wondrous Revelation, this glorious century, the foundation of the Faith of God and the distinguishing feature of His Law is the consciousness of the Oneness of Mankind."

How pathetic indeed are the efforts of those leaders of human institutions who, in utter disregard of the spirit of the age, are striving to adjust national processes, suited to the ancient days of self-contained nations to an age which must either achieve the unity of the world, as adumbrated by Bahá'u'lláh, or perish. At so critical an hour in the history of civilization it behooves the leaders of all the nations of the world, great and small, whether in the East or in the West, whether victors or vanquished, to give heed to the clarion call of Bahá'u'lláh and, thoroughly imbued with a sense of world solidarity, the sine qua non of loyalty to His Cause, arise manfully to carry out in its entirety the one remedial scheme He, the Divine Physician, has prescribed for an ailing humanity. Let them discard, once for all, every preconceived idea, every national prejudice, and give heed to the sublime counsel of 'Abdu'l-Bahá, the authorized Expounder of His teachings. You can best serve your country, was 'Abdu'l-Bahá's rejoinder to a high official in the service of the federal government of the United States of America, who had questioned Him as to the best manner in which he could promote the interests of his government and people, if you strive, in your capacity as a citizen of the world, to assist in the eventual application of the principle of federalism underlying the government of your own country to the relationships now existing between the peoples and nations of the world. (Shoghi Effendi, *The World Order of Bahá'u'lláh*, pp. 36–37)

World unity is the goal towards which a harassed humanity is striving. Nation-building has come to an end. The anarchy inherent in state sovereignty is moving towards a climax. A world, growing to maturity, must abandon this fetish, recognize the oneness and wholeness of human relationships, and establish once for all the machinery that can best incarnate this fundamental principle of its life. (Shoghi Effendi, *The World Order of Bahá'u'lláh*, p. 202)

As we view the world around us, we are compelled to observe the manifold evidences of that universal fermentation which, in every continent of the globe and in every department of human life, be it religious, social, economic or political, is purging and reshaping humanity in anticipation of the Day when the wholeness of the human race will have been recognized and its unity established. A twofold process, however, can be distinguished, each tending, in its own way and with an accelerated momentum, to bring to a climax the forces that are transforming the face of our planet. The first is essentially an integrating process, while the second is fundamentally disruptive. The former, as it steadily evolves, unfolds a System which may well serve as a pattern for that world polity towards which a strangely-disordered world is continually advancing; while the latter, as its disintegrating influence deepens, tends to tear down, with increasing violence, the antiquated barriers that seek to block humanity's progress towards its destined goal. The constructive process stands associated with the nascent Faith of Bahá'u'lláh, and is the harbinger of the New World Order that Faith must erelong establish. The destructive forces that characterize the other should be identified with a civilization that has refused to answer to the expectation of a new age, and is consequently falling into chaos and decline.

A titanic, a spiritual struggle, unparalleled in its magnitude yet unspeakably glorious in its ultimate consequences, is being waged as a result of these opposing tendencies, in this age of transition through which the organized community of the followers of Bahá'u'lláh and mankind as a whole are passing. (Shoghi Effendi, *The World Order of Bahá'u'lláh*, p. 170)

The oneness of humanity, with its corollary of unity in diversity, is applicable both to the peoples and to the nations of the world. It is a practical, indeed, essential standard for ordering humankind's collective life on the planet. The oneness of humanity is at once a statement of principle and the ultimate goal of human existence. It implies more than a willingness to cooperate; it speaks to the longing of people everywhere for a world infused with such a spirit of community, fellowship and compassion that human misery and degradation, violence and oppression will become intolerable and eventually unthinkable. In such a world, peace, social and economic justice, prosperity and liberty will become the order of the day. The growing acceptance of the oneness of humanity is the single most powerful force impelling the world toward unity.

In our increasingly interdependent world, it is no longer possible for a people or a nation to achieve lasting prosperity at the expense of other peoples and nations. (Bahá'í International Community, "Global Action Plan for Social Development")

The right to enjoy an adequate standard of living and the right to development are, indeed, within the reach of nations. Bahá'ís believe that the scientific and technological advances occurring in this momentous century signal a great surge forward in the social evolution of humanity, and provide the means by which its practical problems may be solved. They, in fact, make possible the administration of the complex life of a united world.

Nevertheless, barriers persist. Doubts, misconceptions, prejudices, suspicions and narrow self-interest beset nations and peoples in their relations with one another. Unfortunately, the arbiters of human affairs have, instead of embracing the concept of the oneness of mankind and promoting the increase of concord among different peoples, tended to deify the State, to subordinate the rest of mankind to one nation, race or class, to attempt to suppress all discussion and interchange of ideas, or callously to abandon starving millions to the operations of a market system that all too clearly is aggravating the plight of the majority of mankind, while enabling small sections to live in an unprecedented condition of affluence. (Bahá'í International Community, "Right to Development")

2

FUNDAMENTAL PRINCIPLES FOR THE PEACE AND PROSPERITY OF THE WORLD

As the rich man enjoys his life surrounded by ease and luxuries, so the poor man must, likewise, have a home and be provided with sustenance and comforts commensurate with his needs. This readjustment of the social economy is of the greatest importance inasmuch as it ensures the stability of the world of humanity; and until it is effected, happiness and prosperity are impossible.
—'Abdu'l-Bahá, *The Promulgation of Universal Peace*, p. 252

On Eliminating Extremes of Wealth and Poverty

One of the most important principles of the Teaching of Bahá'u'lláh is:

The right of every human being to the daily bread whereby they exist, or the equalization of the means of livelihood.

The arrangements of the circumstances of the people must be such that poverty shall disappear, that everyone, as far as possible, according to his rank and position, shall share in comfort and well-being. . . .

Certainly, some being enormously rich and others lamentably poor, an organization is necessary to control and improve this state of affairs. It is important to limit riches, as it is also of importance to limit poverty. Either extreme is not good. To be seated in the mean* is most desirable. If it be right

---

* Give me neither poverty nor riches. (King James Bible, Proverbs, Ch. 30, v. 8.)

for a capitalist to possess a large fortune, it is equally just that his workman should have a sufficient means of existence.

A financier with colossal wealth should not exist whilst near him is a poor man in dire necessity. When we see poverty allowed to reach a condition of starvation it is a sure sign that somewhere we shall find tyranny. Men must bestir themselves in this matter, and no longer delay in altering conditions which bring the misery of grinding poverty to a very large number of the people. The rich must give of their abundance, they must soften their hearts and cultivate a compassionate intelligence, taking thought for those sad ones who are suffering from lack of the very necessities of life. ('Abdu'l-Bahá, *Paris Talks*, no. 46.1–3, 10–11)

The Global Formula for Peace and Prosperity

Now concerning our social principles, namely the teachings of His Holiness Bahá'u'lláh spread far and wide fifty years ago, they verily comprehend all other teachings. It is clear and evident that without these teachings progress and advancement for mankind are in no wise possible. Every community in the world findeth in these Divine Teachings the realization of its highest aspirations. These teachings are even as the tree that beareth the best fruits of all trees. Philosophers, for instance, find in these heavenly teachings the most perfect solution of their social problems, and similarly a true and noble exposition of matters that pertain to philosophical questions. In like manner men of faith behold the reality of religion manifestly revealed in these heavenly teachings, and clearly and conclusively prove them to be the real and true remedy for the ills and infirmities of all mankind. Should these sublime teachings be diffused, mankind shall be freed from all perils, from all chronic ills and sicknesses. In like manner are the Bahá'í economic principles the embodiment of the highest aspirations of all wage-earning classes and of economists of various schools. ('Abdu'l-Bahá, *Tablet to August Forel*, p. 26)

Bahá'u'lláh has risen from the eastern horizon. Like the glory of the sun He has come into the world. He has reflected the reality of divine religion, dispelled the darkness of imitations, laid the foundation of new teachings and resuscitated the world.

The first teaching of Bahá'u'lláh is the investigation of reality. Man must seek reality himself, forsaking imitations and adherence to mere hereditary forms. As the nations of the world are following imitations in lieu of truth and as imitations are many and various, differences of belief have been productive of strife and warfare. So long as these imitations remain, the oneness of the world of humanity is impossible. Therefore, we must investigate reality in order that by its light the clouds and darkness may be dispelled. Reality is one reality; it does not admit multiplicity or division. If the nations of the world investigate reality, they will agree and become united. . . .

The second teaching of Bahá'u'lláh concerns the unity of mankind. All are the servants of God and members of one human family. God has created all, and all are His children. He rears, nourishes, provides for and is kind to all. Why should we be unjust and unkind? This is the policy of God, the lights of which have shone throughout the world. His sun bestows its effulgence unsparingly upon all; His clouds send down rain without distinction or favor; His breezes refresh the whole earth. It is evident that humankind without exception is sheltered beneath His mercy and protection. Some are imperfect; they must be perfected. The ignorant must be taught, the sick healed, the sleepers awakened. The child must not be oppressed or censured because it is undeveloped; it must be patiently trained. The sick must not be neglected because they are ailing; nay, rather, we must have compassion upon them and bring them healing. Briefly, the old conditions of animosity, bigotry and hatred between the religious systems must be dispelled and the new conditions of love, agreement and spiritual brotherhood be established among them.

The third teaching of Bahá'u'lláh is that religion must be the source of fellowship, the cause of unity and the nearness of God to man. If it rouses hatred and strife, it is evident that absence of religion is preferable and an irreligious man better than one who professes it. According to the divine Will and intention religion should be the cause of love and agreement, a bond to unify all mankind, for it is a message of peace and goodwill to man from God.

The fourth teaching of Bahá'u'lláh is the agreement of religion and science. God has endowed man with intelligence and reason whereby he is required to determine the verity of questions and propositions. If religious beliefs and opinions are found contrary to the standards of science, they are mere superstitions and imaginations; for the antithesis of knowledge is ignorance, and the child of ignorance is superstition. Unquestionably there must be agreement between true religion and science. If a question be found contrary to reason, faith and belief in it are impossible, and there is no outcome but wavering and vacillation.

Bahá'u'lláh also taught that prejudices—whether religious, racial, patriotic or political—are destructive to the foundations of human development. Prejudices of any kind are the destroyers of human happiness and welfare. Until they are dispelled, the advancement of the world of humanity is not possible; yet racial, religious and national biases are observed everywhere. For thousands of years the world of humanity has been agitated and disturbed by prejudices. As long as it prevails, warfare, animosity and hatred will continue. Therefore, if we seek to establish peace, we must cast aside this obstacle; for otherwise, agreement and composure are not to be attained.

Sixth, Bahá'u'lláh set forth principles of guidance and teaching for economic readjustment. Regulations were revealed by Him which ensure the welfare of the commonwealth. As the rich man enjoys his life surrounded by ease and luxuries, so the poor man must, likewise, have a home and be provided with sustenance and comforts commensurate with his needs. This readjustment of the social economy is of the greatest importance inasmuch as it ensures the stability of the world of humanity; and until it is effected, happiness and prosperity are impossible.

Seventh, Bahá'u'lláh taught that an equal standard of human rights must be recognized and adopted. In the estimation of God all men are equal; there is no distinction or preferment for any soul in the dominion of His justice and equity.

Eighth, education is essential, and all standards of training and teaching throughout the world of mankind should be brought into conformity and agreement; a universal curriculum should be established, and the basis of ethics be the same.

Ninth, a universal language shall be adopted and be taught by all the schools and institutions of the world. A committee appointed by national bodies of learning shall select a suitable language to be used as a medium of international communication. All must acquire it. This is one of the great factors in the unification of man.

Tenth, Bahá'u'lláh emphasized and established the equality of man and woman. Sex is not particularized to humanity; it exists throughout the animate kingdoms but without distinction or preference. In the vegetable kingdom there is complete equality between male and female of species. Likewise, in the animal plane equality exists; all are under the protection of God. Is it becoming to man that he, the noblest of creatures, should observe and insist upon such distinction? Woman's lack of progress and proficiency has been due to her need of equal education and opportunity. Had she been allowed this equality, there is no doubt she would be the counterpart of man in ability and capacity. The happiness of mankind will be realized when women and men coordinate and advance equally, for each is the complement and helpmeet of the other. ('Abdu'l-Bahá, *The Promulgation of Universal Peace*, pp. 250–53)

The Bahá'í Faith upholds the unity of God, recognizes the unity of His Prophets, and inculcates the principle of the oneness and wholeness of the entire human race. It proclaims the necessity and the inevitability of the unification of mankind, asserts that it is gradually approaching, and claims that nothing short of the transmuting spirit of God, working through His chosen Mouthpiece in this day, can ultimately succeed in bringing it about. . . . It unequivocally maintains the principle of equal rights, opportunities and privileges for men and women, insists on compulsory education, eliminates extremes of poverty and wealth, . . . prohibits slavery, asceticism, mendicancy and monasticism, . . . emphasizes the necessity of strict obedience to one's government, exalts any work performed in the spirit of service to the level of worship, . . . and delineates the outlines of those institutions that must establish and perpetuate the general peace of mankind. (From a Statement by Shoghi Effendi, dated 14 July 1947, addressed to a United Nations Commission)

Coherence between the Spiritual and the Material

. . . until material achievements, physical accomplishments and human virtues are reinforced by spiritual perfections, luminous qualities and characteristics of mercy, no fruit or result shall issue therefrom, nor will the happiness of the world of humanity, which is the ultimate aim, be attained. For although, on the one hand, material achievements and the development of the physical world produce prosperity, which exquisitely manifests its intended aims, on the other hand dangers, severe calamities and violent afflictions are imminent.

Consequently, when thou lookest at the orderly pattern of kingdoms, cities and villages, with the attractiveness of their adornments, the freshness of their natural resources, the refinement of their appliances, the ease of their means of travel, the extent of knowledge available about the world of nature, the great inventions, the colossal enterprises, the noble discoveries and scientific researches, thou wouldst conclude that civilization conduceth to the happiness and the progress of the human world. Yet shouldst thou turn thine eye to the discovery of destructive and infernal machines, to the development of forces of demolition and the invention of fiery implements, which uproot the tree of life, it would become evident and manifest unto thee that civilization is conjoined with barbarism. Progress and barbarism go hand in hand, unless material civilization be confirmed by Divine Guidance, by the revelations of the All-Merciful and by godly virtues, and be reinforced by spiritual conduct, by the ideals of the Kingdom and by the outpourings of the Realm of Might.

Consider now, that the most advanced and civilized countries of the world have been turned into arsenals of explosives, that the continents of the globe have been transformed into huge camps and battlefields, that the peoples of the world have formed themselves into armed nations, and that the governments of the world are vying with each other as to who will first step into the field of carnage and bloodshed, thus subjecting mankind to the utmost degree of affliction.

Therefore, this civilization and material progress should be combined with the Most Great Guidance so that this nether world may become the scene of the appearance of the bestowals of the Kingdom, and physical achievements may be conjoined with the effulgences of the Merciful. This in order that the beauty and perfection of the world of man may be unveiled and be manifested before all in the utmost grace and splendor. Thus everlasting glory and happiness shall be revealed. ('Abdu'l-Bahá, *Selections from the Writings of 'Abdu'l-Bahá*, no. 225.5–9)

For the world is dark with discord and selfishness, hearts are negligent, souls are bereft of God and His heavenly bestowals. Man is submerged in the affairs of this world. His aims, objects and attainments are mortal, whereas God desires for him immortal accomplishments. In his heart there is no thought of God. He has sacrificed his portion and birthright of divine spirituality. Desire and passion, like two unmanageable horses, have wrested the reins of control from him and are galloping madly in the wilderness. This is the cause of the degradation of the world of humanity. This is the cause of its retrogression into the appetites and passions of the animal kingdom. Instead of divine advancement we find sensual captivity and debasement of heavenly virtues of the soul. By devotion to the carnal, mortal world human susceptibilities sink to the level of animalism. ('Abdu'l-Bahá, *The Promulgation of Universal Peace*, p. 256)

This all shows that material progress alone does not tend to uplift man. On the contrary, the more he becomes immersed in material progress, the more does his spirituality become obscured. ('Abdu'l-Bahá, *Paris Talks*, no. 34.4)

Progress is of two kinds: material and spiritual. The former is attained through observation of the surrounding existence and constitutes the foundation of civilization. Spiritual progress is through the breaths of the Holy Spirit and is the awakening of the conscious soul of man to perceive the reality of Divinity. Material progress ensures the happiness of the human world. Spiritual progress ensures the happiness and eternal continuance of the soul. The Prophets of God have founded the laws of divine civilization. They have been the root and fundamental source of all knowledge. They have established the principles of human brotherhood, of fraternity, which is of various kinds—such as the fraternity of family, of race, of nation and of ethical motives. These forms of fraternity, these bonds of brotherhood, are merely temporal and transient in association. They do not ensure harmony and are usually productive of disagreement. They do not prevent warfare and strife; on the contrary, they are selfish, restricted and fruitful causes of enmity and hatred among mankind. The spiritual brotherhood which is enkindled and established through the breaths of the Holy Spirit unites nations and removes the cause of warfare and strife. It transforms mankind into one great family and establishes the foundations of the oneness of humanity. It promulgates the spirit of international agreement and ensures universal peace. Therefore, we must investigate the foundation of this heavenly fraternity. We must forsake all imitations and promote the reality of the divine teachings. In accordance with these principles and actions and by the assistance of the Holy Spirit, both material and spiritual happiness shall become realized. Until all nations and peoples become united by the bonds of the Holy Spirit in this real fraternity, until national and international prejudices are effaced in the reality of this spiritual brotherhood, true progress, prosperity and lasting happiness will not be attained by man. ('Abdu'l-Bahá, *The Promulgation of Universal Peace*, pp. 194–95)

Undeniably, poverty is sustained by an interaction of social and material factors. This interaction determines the societal benefits of material resources, whether the resources are concentrated in the hands of a few or are equitably distributed, whether they are beneficial or harmful to the society at large. Today, much of economic activity and its institutional context is at odds with environmental sustainability, the advancement of women, the well-being of the family, the engagement of young people, the availability of employment, and the expansion of knowledge. . . . The economic theories of impersonal markets, promoting self-centered actions of individuals, have not helped humanity escape the extremes of poverty on the one hand and over-consumption on the other. New economic theories for our time must be animated by a motive beyond just profit. They must be rooted in the very human and relational dimension of all economic activity, which binds us as families, as communities and as citizens of one world. They must be animated by a spirit of innovation rather than blind imitation, ennoblement rather than exploitation, and the full and confident participation of women. (Bahá'í International Community, *Eradicating Poverty: Moving Forward as One*)

Among the elements most relevant to social action are statements that define the character of progress—that civilization has both a material and a spiritual dimension, that humanity is on the threshold of its collective maturity, that there are destructive and constructive forces operating in the world which serve to propel humanity along the path towards its full maturity, that the relationships necessary to sustain society must be recast in the light of Bahá'u'lláh's Revelation, that the transformation required must occur simultaneously within human consciousness and the structure of social institutions. . . .

An exploration of the nature of social action, undertaken from a Bahá'í perspective, must necessarily place it in the broad context of the advancement of civilization. That a global civilization which is both materially and spiritually prosperous represents the next stage of a millennia-long process of social evolution provides a conception of history that endows every instance of social action with a particular purpose: to foster true prosperity, with its spiritual and material dimensions, among the diverse inhabitants of the planet. A concept of vital relevance, then, is the imperative to achieve a dynamic coherence between the practical and spiritual requirements of life. 'Abdu'l-Bahá states that while "material civilization is one of the means for the progress of the world of mankind," until it is "combined with Divine civilization, the desired result, which is the felicity of mankind, will not be attained." He continues:

> Material civilization is like a lamp-glass. Divine civilization is the lamp itself and the glass without the light is dark. Material civilization is like the body. No matter how infinitely graceful, elegant and beautiful it may be, it is dead. Divine civilization is like the spirit, and the body gets its life from the spirit, otherwise it becomes a corpse. It has thus been made evident that the world of mankind is in need of the breaths of the Holy Spirit. Without the spirit the world of mankind is lifeless, and without this light the world of mankind is in utter darkness.

To seek coherence between the spiritual and the material does not imply that the material goals of development are to be trivialized. It does require, however, the rejection of approaches to development which define it as the transfer to all societies of the ideological convictions, the social structures, the economic practices, the models of governance—in the final analysis, the very patterns of life—prevalent in certain highly industrialized regions of the world. When the material and spiritual dimensions of the life of a community are kept in mind and due attention is given to both scientific and spiritual knowledge, the tendency to reduce development to the mere consumption of goods and services and the naive use of technological packages is avoided. Scientific knowledge, to take but one simple example, helps the members of a community to analyse the physical and social implications of a given technological proposal—say, its environmental impact—and spiritual insight gives rise to moral imperatives that uphold social harmony and that ensure technology serves the common good. Together, these two sources of knowledge tap roots of motivation in individuals and communities, so essential in breaking free from the shelter of passivity, and enable them to uncover the traps of consumerism.

Although the relevance of scientific knowledge to development efforts is readily acknowledged in the world at large, there appears to be less agreement on the part to be played by religion. Too often views about religion carry with them notions of division, strife, and repression, creating a reluctance to turn to it as a source of knowledge—even among those who question the adequacy of entirely materialistic approaches. Interestingly, the high esteem in which science is held does not necessarily imply that its practice and purpose are well understood. Its underlying meaning, too, is surrounded by misconception. Not infrequently it is conceived in terms of the application of certain techniques and formulas, which, as if by magic, lead to this or that effect. It is not surprising, then, that what is considered to be religious knowledge is not in harmony with science, and much of what is propagated in the name of science denies the spiritual capacities cultivated by religion.

Social action, of whatever size and complexity, should strive to remain free of simplistic and distorted conceptions of science and religion. To this end, an imaginary duality between reason and faith—a duality that would confine reason to the realm of empirical evidence and logical argumentation and which would associate faith with superstition and irrational thought—must be avoided. The process of development has to be rational and systematic— incorporating, for example, scientific capabilities of observing, of measuring, of rigorously testing ideas—and at the same time deeply aware of faith and spiritual convictions. In the words of 'Abdu'l-Bahá: "faith compriseth both knowledge and the performance of good works." Faith and reason can best be understood as attributes of the human soul through which insights and knowledge can be gained about the physical and the spiritual dimensions of existence. They make it possible to recognize the powers and capacities latent in individuals and in humanity as a whole and enable people to work for the realization of these potentialities.

The following passage written by the Universal House of Justice provides guidance in this connection:

Bahá'u'lláh's Revelation is vast. It calls for profound change not only at the level of the individual but also in the structure of society. "Is not the object of every Revelation," He Himself proclaims, "to effect a transformation in the whole character of mankind, a transformation that shall manifest itself, both outwardly and inwardly, that shall affect both its inner life and external conditions?" The work advancing in every corner of the globe today represents the latest stage of the ongoing Bahá'í endeavour to create the nucleus of the glorious civilization enshrined in His teachings, the building of which is an enterprise of infinite complexity and scale, one that will demand centuries of exertion by humanity to bring to fruition. There are no shortcuts, no formulas. Only as effort is made to draw on insights from His Revelation, to tap into the accumulating knowledge of the human race, to apply His teachings intelligently to the life of humanity, and to consult on the questions that arise will the necessary learning occur and capacity be developed.

(*Social Action*, A paper prepared by the Office of Social and Economic Development at the Bahá'í World Center, 26 November 2012)

The Source of Moral Conviction
If the edifice of religion shakes and totters, commotion and chaos will ensue and the order of things will be utterly upset, for in the world of mankind there are two safeguards that protect man from wrong-doing. One is the law which punishes the criminal; but the law prevents only the manifest crime and not the concealed sin; whereas the ideal safeguard, namely, the religion of God, prevents both the manifest and the concealed crime, trains man, educates morals, compels the adoption of virtues and is the all-inclusive power which guarantees the felicity of the world of mankind. But by religion is meant that which is ascertained by investigation and not that which is base on mere imitation, the foundation of Divine Religions and not human imitations. ('Abdu'l-Bahá, Tablet to the Hague)

A Greek philosopher living in the days of the youth of Christianity, being full of the Christian element, though not a professing Christian, wrote thus: "It is my belief that religion is the very foundation of true civilization." For, unless the moral character of a nation is educated, as well as its brain and its talents, civilization has no sure basis.

As religion inculcates morality, it is therefore the truest philosophy, and on it is built the only lasting civilization. As an example of this, he points out the Christians of the time whose morality was on a very high level. The belief of this philosopher conforms to the truth, for the civilization of Christianity was the best and most enlightened in the world. The Christian Teaching was illumined by the Divine Sun of Truth, therefore its followers were taught to love all men as brothers to fear nothing, not even death! To love their neighbors as themselves, and to forget their own selfish interests in striving for the greater good of humanity. The grand aim of the religion of Christ was to draw the hearts of all men nearer to God's effulgent Truth. ('Abdu'l-Bahá, *Paris Talks,* no. 7.3–4)

If we investigate the religions to discover the principles underlying their foundations, we will find they agree; for the fundamental reality of them is one and not multiple. By this means the religionists of the world will reach their point of unity and reconciliation. They will ascertain the truth that the purpose of religion is the acquisition of praiseworthy virtues, the betterment of morals, the spiritual development of mankind, the real life and divine bestowals. All the Prophets have been the promoters of these principles; none of Them has been the promoter of corruption, vice or evil. They have summoned mankind to all good. They have united people in the love of God, invited them to the religions of the unity of mankind and exhorted them to amity and agreement. ('Abdu'l-Bahá, *The Promulgation of Universal Peace,* p. 210)

Likewise, in the spiritual realm of intelligence and idealism there must be a center of illumination, and that center is the everlasting, ever-shining

Sun, the Word of God. Its lights are the lights of reality which have shone upon humanity, illumining the realm of thought and morals, conferring the bounties of the divine world upon man. These lights are the cause of the education of souls and the source of the enlightenment of hearts, sending forth in effulgent radiance the message of the glad tidings of the Kingdom of God. In brief, the moral and ethical world and the world of spiritual regeneration are dependent for their progressive being upon that heavenly Center of illumination. It gives forth the light of religion and bestows the life of the spirit, imbues humanity with archetypal virtues and confers eternal splendors. This Sun of Reality, this Center of effulgences, is the Prophet or Manifestation of God. Just as the phenomenal sun shines upon the material world producing life and growth, likewise, the spiritual or prophetic Sun confers illumination upon the human world of thought and intelligence, and unless it rose upon the horizon of human existence, the kingdom of man would become dark and extinguished. ('Abdu'l-Bahá, *The Promulgation of Universal Peace*, p. 130)

The exigencies of the new age of human experience to which Bahá'u'lláh summoned the political and religious rulers of the nineteenth century world have now been largely adopted, at least as ideals, by their successors and by progressive minds everywhere. By the time the twentieth century had drawn to a close, principles that had, only short decades earlier, been patronized as visionary and hopelessly unrealistic had become central to global discourse. Buttressed by the findings of scientific research and the conclusions of influential commissions—often lavishly funded—they direct the work of powerful agencies at international, national and local levels. A vast body of scholarly literature in many languages is devoted to exploring practical means for their implementation, and those programmes can count on media attention on five continents.

Most of these principles are, alas, also widely flouted, not only among recognized enemies of social peace, but in circles professedly committed to them. What is lacking is not convincing testimony as to their relevance, but the power of moral conviction that can implement them, a power whose only demonstrably reliable source throughout history has been religious faith. As late as the inception of Bahá'u'lláh's own mission, religious authority still exercised a significant degree of social influence. When the Christian world was moved to break with millennia of unquestioning conviction and address at last the evil of slavery, it was to Biblical ideals that the early British reformers sought to appeal. Subsequently, in the defining address he gave regarding the central role played by the issue in the great conflict in America, the president of the United States warned that if "every drop of blood drawn with the lash shall be paid by another drawn with the sword, as was said three thousand years ago, so still it must be said 'the judgements of the Lord are true and righteous altogether.'"* That era, however, was swiftly drawing to a close. In the upheavals that followed the Second World War, even so influential a figure as Mohandas Gandhi proved unable to mobilize the spiritual power of Hinduism in support of his efforts to extinguish sectarian violence on the Indian subcontinent. Nor were leaders of the Islamic community any more effective in this respect. As prefigured in the Qur'án's metaphorical vision of "The Day that We roll up the heavens like a scroll,"** the once unchallengeable authority of the traditional religions had ceased to direct humanity's social relations.

It is in this context that one begins to appreciate Bahá'u'lláh's choice of imagery about the will of God for a new age: "Think not that We have revealed unto you a mere code of laws. Nay, rather, We have unsealed the choice Wine with the fingers of might and power." Through His revelation, the principles required for the collective coming of age of the human race have been invested with the one power capable of penetrating to the roots of human motivation and of altering behaviour. For those who have recognized Him, equality of men and women is not a sociological postulate,

---

* Abraham Lincoln, quoted in *Inaugural Addresses of the Presidents of the United States* (Washington, D.C.: U.S. Government Printing Office, 1989).

** Qur'án, 21:104.

but revealed truth about human nature, with implications for every aspect of human relations. The same is true of His teaching of the principle of racial oneness. Universal education, freedom of thought, the protection of human rights, recognition of the earth's vast resources as a trust for the whole of humankind, society's responsibility for the well-being of its citizenry, the promotion of scientific research, even so practical a principle as an international auxiliary language that will advance integration of the earth's peoples—for all who respond to Bahá'u'lláh's revelation, these and similar precepts carry the same compelling authority as do the injunctions of scripture against idolatry, theft and false witness. While intimations of some can be perceived in earlier sacred writings, their definition and prescription had necessarily to wait until the planet's heterogeneous populations could set out together on the discovery of their nature as a single human race. Through spiritual empowerment brought by Bahá'u'lláh's revelation the Divine standards can be appreciated, not as isolated principles and laws, but as facets of a single, all-embracing vision of humanity's future, revolutionary in purpose, intoxicating in the possibilities it opens. (Prepared under the supervision of the Universal House of Justice, *One Common Faith*, pp. 38–40)

Throughout recorded history, human consciousness has depended upon two basic knowledge systems through which its potentialities have progressively been expressed: science and religion. Through these two agencies, the race's experience has been organized, its environment interpreted, its latent powers explored, and its moral and intellectual life disciplined. It is, therefore, in the context of raising the level of human capacity through the expansion of knowledge at all levels that the economic issues facing humankind need to be addressed. Instruments of social and economic change so powerful must cease to be the patrimony of advantaged segments of society, and must be so organized as to permit people everywhere to participate in such activity on the basis of capacity.

Moreover, as the experience of recent decades has demonstrated, material benefits and endeavors cannot be regarded as ends in themselves. Their value consists not only in providing for humanity's basic needs in housing, food, health care, and the like, but in extending the reach of human abilities. The most important role that economic efforts must play in development lies, therefore, in equipping people and institutions with the means through which they can achieve the real purpose of development: that is, laying foundations for a new social order that can cultivate the limitless potentialities latent in human consciousness.

Only in this way can economics and the related sciences free themselves from the undertow of the materialistic preoccupations that now distract them, and fulfil their potential as tools vital to achieving human well-being in the full sense of the term. Nowhere is the need for a rigorous dialogue between the work of science and the insights of religion more apparent.

The problem of poverty is a case in point. Proposals aimed at addressing it are predicated on the conviction that material resources exist, or can be created by scientific and technological endeavour, which will alleviate and eventually entirely eradicate this age-old condition as a feature of human life. A major reason why such relief is not achieved is that the necessary scientific and technological advances respond to a set of priorities only tangentially related to the real interests of the generality of humankind. A radical reordering of these priorities will be required if the burden of poverty is finally to be lifted from the world. Such an achievement demands a determined quest for appropriate values, a quest that will test profoundly both the spiritual and scientific resources of humankind. Religion will be severely hampered in contributing to this joint undertaking so long as it is held prisoner by sectarian doctrines which cannot distinguish between contentment and mere passivity and which teach that poverty is an inherent feature of earthly life, escape from which lies only in the world beyond. To participate effectively in the struggle to bring material well-being to humanity, the religious spirit must find—in the Source of inspiration from which it flows—new spiritual concepts and principles relevant to an age that seeks to establish unity and justice in human affairs. (Bahá'í International Community, *The Prosperity of Humankind*)

Institutional Framework for a Just and Secure Order

The unity of the human race, as envisaged by Bahá'u'lláh, implies the establishment of a world commonwealth in which all nations, races, creeds and classes are closely and permanently united, and in which the autonomy of its state members and the personal freedom and initiative of the individuals that compose them are definitely and completely safeguarded. This commonwealth must, as far as we can visualize it, consist of a world legislature, whose members will, as the trustees of the whole of mankind, ultimately control the entire resources of all the component nations, and will enact such laws as shall be required to regulate the life, satisfy the needs and adjust the relationships of all races and peoples. A world executive, backed by an international Force, will carry out the decisions arrived at, and apply the laws enacted by, this world legislature, and will safeguard the organic unity of the whole commonwealth. A world tribunal will adjudicate and deliver its compulsory and final verdict in all and any disputes that may arise between the various elements constituting this universal system. A mechanism of world inter-communication will be devised, embracing the whole planet, freed from national hindrances and restrictions, and functioning with marvelous swiftness and perfect regularity. A world metropolis will act as the nerve center of a world civilization, the focus towards which the unifying forces of life will converge and from which its energizing influences will radiate. A world language will either be invented or chosen from among the existing languages and will be taught in the schools of all the federated nations as an auxiliary to their mother tongue. A world script, a world literature, a uniform and universal system of currency, of weights and measures, will simplify and facilitate intercourse and understanding among the nations and races of mankind. In such a world society, science and religion, the two most potent forces in human life, will be reconciled, will cooperate, and will harmoniously develop. The press will, under such a system, while giving full scope to the expression of the diversified views and convictions of mankind, cease to be mischievously manipulated by vested interests, whether private or public, and will be liberated from the influence of contending governments and peoples. The economic resources of the world will be organized, its sources of raw materials will be tapped and fully utilized, its markets will be coordinated and developed, and the distribution of its products will be equitably regulated.

National rivalries, hatreds, and intrigues will cease, and racial animosity and prejudice will be replaced by racial amity, understanding and cooperation. The causes of religious strife will be permanently removed, economic barriers and restrictions will be completely abolished, and the inordinate distinction between classes will be obliterated. Destitution on the one hand, and gross accumulation of ownership on the other, will disappear. The enormous energy dissipated and wasted on war, whether economic or political, will be consecrated to such ends as will extend the range of human inventions and technical development, to the increase of the productivity of mankind, to the extermination of disease, to the extension of scientific research, to the raising of the standard of physical health, to the sharpening and refinement of the human brain, to the exploitation of the unused and unsuspected resources of the planet, to the prolongation of human life, and to the furtherance of any other agency that can stimulate the intellectual, the moral, and spiritual life of the entire human race.

A world federal system, ruling the whole earth and exercising unchallengeable authority over its unimaginably vast resources, blending and embodying the ideals of both the East and the West, liberated from the curse of war and its miseries, and bent on the exploitation of all the available sources of energy on the surface of the planet, a system in which Force is made the servant of Justice, whose life is sustained by its universal recognition of one God and by its allegiance to one common Revelation—such is the goal towards which humanity, impelled by the unifying forces of life, is moving. (Shoghi Effendi, *The World Order of Bahá'u'lláh*, pp. 203–4)

Some form of a world super-state must needs be evolved, in whose favor all the nations of the world will have willingly ceded every claim to make war, certain rights to impose taxation and all rights to maintain armaments, except for purposes of maintaining internal order within their respective dominions. Such a state will have to include within its orbit an international executive adequate to enforce supreme and unchallengeable authority on every recalcitrant member of the commonwealth; a world parliament whose members shall be elected by the people in their respective countries and whose election shall be confirmed by their respective governments; and a supreme tribunal whose judgement will have a binding effect even in such cases where the parties concerned did not voluntarily agree to submit their case to its consideration. A world community in which all economic barriers will have been permanently demolished and the interdependence of Capital and Labor definitely recognized; in which the clamor of religious fanaticism and strife will have been for ever stilled; in which the flame of racial animosity will have been finally extinguished; in which a single code of international law—the product of the considered judgement of the world's federated representatives—shall have as its sanction the instant and coercive intervention of the combined forces of the federated units; and finally a world community in which the fury of a capricious and militant nationalism will have been transmuted into an abiding consciousness of world citizenship—such indeed, appears, in its broadest outline, the Order anticipated by Bahá'u'lláh, an Order that shall come to be regarded as the fairest fruit of a slowly maturing age.

"The Tabernacle of Unity," Bahá'u'lláh proclaims in His message to all mankind, "has been raised; regard ye not one another as strangers. . . . Of one tree are all ye the fruit and of one bough the leaves. . . . The world is but one country and mankind its citizens. . . . Let not a man glory in that he loves his country; let him rather glory in this, that he loves his kind." (Shoghi Effendi, *The World Order of Bahá'u'lláh,* pp. 40–41)

It is now increasingly acknowledged that such conditions as the marginalization of girls and women, poor governance, ethnic and religious antipathy, environmental degradation and unemployment constitute formidable obstacles to the progress and development of communities. These evidence a deeper crisis—one rooted in the values and attitudes that shape relationships at all levels of society. Viewed from this perspective, poverty can be described as the absence of those ethical, social and material resources needed to develop the moral, intellectual and social capacities of individuals, communities and institutions. Moral reasoning, group decision-making and freedom from racism, for example, are all essential tools for poverty alleviation. Such capacities must shape individual thinking as well as institutional arrangements and policy-making. To be clear, the goal at hand is not only to remove the ills of poverty but to engage the masses of humanity in the construction of a just global order. (The Bahá'í International Community, "Eradicating Poverty: Moving Forward as One")

3

SPIRITUAL AND PRACTICAL FOUNDATIONS FOR A JUST ECONOMIC SYSTEM

Know ye, verily, that the happiness of mankind lieth in the unity and the harmony of the human race, and that spiritual and material developments are conditioned upon love and amity among all men.

—'Abdu'l-Bahá, *Selections from the Writings of 'Abdu'l-Bahá*, no. 225.10

Individual and Collective Transformation through Application of Spiritual Principles

The well-being of mankind, its peace and security, are unattainable unless and until its unity is firmly established. This unity can never be achieved so long as the counsels which the Pen of the Most High hath revealed are suffered to pass unheeded. (Bahá'u'lláh, *Gleanings from the Writings of Bahá'u'lláh*, no. 131.2)

As preordained by the Fountainhead of Creation, the temple of the world hath been fashioned after the image and likeness of the human body. In fact each mirroreth forth the image of the other, wert thou but to observe with discerning eyes. By this is meant that even as the human body in this world which is outwardly composed of different limbs and organs, is in reality a closely integrated, coherent entity, similarly the structure of the physical world is like unto a single being whose limbs and members are inseparably linked together.

Were one to observe with an eye that discovereth the realities of all things, it would become clear that the greatest relationship that bindeth the world of being together lieth in the range of created things themselves, and that co-operation, mutual aid and reciprocity are essential characteristics in the unified body of the world of being, inasmuch as all created things are closely related together and each is influenced by the other or deriveth benefit therefrom, either directly or indirectly.

Consider for instance how one group of created things constituteth the vegetable kingdom, and another the animal kingdom. Each of these two maketh use of certain elements in the air on which its own life dependeth, while each increaseth the quantity of such elements as are essential for the life of the other. In other words, the growth and development of the vegetable world is impossible without the existence of the animal kingdom, and the maintenance of animal life is inconceivable without the co-operation of the vegetable kingdom. Of like kind are the relationships that exist among all created things. Hence it was stated that cooperation and reciprocity are essential properties which are inherent in the unified system of the world of existence, and without which the entire creation would be reduced to nothingness.

In surveying the vast range of creation thou shalt perceive that the higher a kingdom of created things is on the arc of ascent, the more conspicuous are the signs and evidences of the truth that co-operation and reciprocity at the level of a higher order are greater than those that exist at the level of a lower order. For example the evident signs of this fundamental reality are more discernible in the vegetable kingdom than in the mineral, and still more manifest in the animal world than in the vegetable.

And thus when contemplating the human world thou beholdest this wondrous phenomenon shining resplendent from all sides with the utmost perfection, inasmuch as in this station acts of cooperation, mutual assistance and reciprocity are not confined to the body and to things that pertain to the material world, but for all conditions, whether physical or spiritual, such as those related to minds, thoughts, opinions, manners, customs, attitudes,

SPIRITUAL AND PRACTICAL FOUNDATIONS
FOR A JUST ECONOMIC SYSTEM

understandings, feelings or other human susceptibilities. In all these thou shouldst find these binding relationships securely established. The more this interrelationship is strengthened and expanded, the more will human society advance in progress and prosperity. Indeed without these vital ties it would be wholly impossible for the world of humanity to attain true felicity and success. ('Abdu'l-Bahá, in *The Compilation of Compilations,* vol. I, no. 1151)

Again, Bahá'u'lláh declares that all forms of prejudice among mankind must be abandoned and that until existing prejudices are entirely removed, the world of humanity will not and cannot attain peace, prosperity and composure. This principle cannot be found in any other sacred volume than the teachings of Bahá'u'lláh. ('Abdu'l-Bahá, *The Promulgation of Universal Peace,* pp. 611–12)

The fundamentals of the whole economic condition are divine in nature and are associated with the world of the heart and spirit. This is fully explained in the Bahá'í teaching, and without knowledge of its principles no improvement in the economic state can be realized . . . but not through sedition and appeal to physical force—not through warfare, but welfare. ('Abdu'l-Bahá, *The Promulgation of Universal Peace,* p. 334)

The Cause is not an economic system, nor its Founders be considered as having been technical economists. The contribution of the Faith to this subject is essentially indirect, as it consists of the application of spiritual principles to our present-day economic system. Bahá'u'lláh has given us a few basic principles which should guide future Bahá'í economists in establishing such institutions which will adjust the economic relationships of the world. . . . (Shoghi Effendi, *Directives from the Guardian,* p. 20)

By the statement "the economic solution is divine in nature" is meant that religion alone can, in the last resort, bring in man's nature such a fundamental change as to enable him to adjust the economic relationships of society. It is only in this way that man can control the economic forces that threaten to disrupt the foundations of his existence, and thus assert his mastery over the forces of nature. (From a letter written on behalf of Shoghi Effendi, dated 26 December 1935, to an individual believer, in *Wealth: Redistribution of*)

World order can be founded only on an unshakeable consciousness of the oneness of mankind, a spiritual truth which all the human sciences confirm. Anthropology, physiology, psychology, recognize only one human species, albeit infinitely varied in the secondary aspects of life. Recognition of this truth requires abandonment of prejudice—prejudice of every kind—race, class, color, creed, nation, sex, degree of material civilization, everything which enables people to consider themselves superior to others. (The Universal House of Justice, *The Promise of World Peace*, ¶39)

Humanity's crying need will not be met by a struggle among competing ambitions or by protest against one or another of the countless wrongs afflicting a desperate age. It calls, rather, for a fundamental change of consciousness, for a wholehearted embrace of Bahá'u'lláh's teaching that the time has come when each human being on earth must learn to accept responsibility for the welfare of the entire human family. (The Universal House of Justice, letter dated 24 May 2001, to the Believers Gathered for the Events Marking the Completion of the Projects on Mount Carmel)

The solution to these problems lies not so much in the formulation of workable theories; it is related to the overall spiritual transformation which is to take place through the gradual influence of the Bahá'í teachings on the lives of people throughout the world—a transformation which will itself be the matrix for the solution so anxiously sought. In the meantime, governments, through hard experience, will, no doubt, take steps which are in harmony with the progressive spirit of the times. (The Universal House of Justice, letter dated 6 July 1989, "Economics, Agriculture, and Related Subjects")

Social justice will be attained only when every member of society enjoys a relative degree of material prosperity and gives due regard to the acquisition of spiritual qualities. The solution, then, to prevailing economic difficulties is to be sought as much in the application of spiritual principles as in the implementation of scientific methods and approaches. The family unit offers an ideal setting within which can be shaped those moral attributes that contribute to an appropriate view of material wealth and its utilization.

Referring to the exigencies of the material world, Bahá'u'lláh has affirmed that to every end has been assigned a means for its accomplishment. A natural conclusion to be drawn from reflection on this fundamental principle is that vigilance must be exercised in distinguishing "means" from "ends"; otherwise, what is intended as a mere instrument could easily become the very goal of an individual's life. The acquisition of wealth is a case in point; it is acceptable and praiseworthy to the extent that it serves as a means for achieving higher ends—for meeting one's basic necessities, for fostering the progress of one's family, for promoting the welfare of society, and for contributing to the establishment of a world civilization. But to make the accumulation of wealth the central purpose of one's life is unworthy of any human being.

An idea closely related to the above, and well in accord with the spirit of the Bahá'í teachings, is that the end does not serve to justify the means. However constructive and noble the goal, however significant to one's life or to the welfare of one's family, it must not be attained through improper means. Regrettably, a number of today's leaders—political, social, and religious—as well as some of the directors of financial markets, executives of multinational corporations, chiefs of commerce and industry, and ordinary people who succumb to social pressure and ignore the call of their conscience, act against this principle; they justify any means in order to achieve their goals.

The legitimacy of wealth depends, 'Abdu'l-Bahá has indicated, on how it is acquired and on how it is expended. In this connection, He has stated that "wealth is praiseworthy in the highest degree, if it is acquired by an individual's own efforts and the grace of God, in commerce, agriculture, crafts and industry," if the measures adopted by the individual in generating wealth serve to "enrich the generality of the people," and if the wealth thus obtained is expended for "philanthropic purposes" and "the promotion of knowledge," for the establishment of schools and industry and the advancement of education, and in general for the welfare of society.

Reflect on the significance of 'Abdu'l-Bahá's words, at once complex and subtle. Quite apart from the already formidable obstacles to employment and service that certain fanatical elements have placed in your path, a host of negative forces, generated by the materialism and corruption so widespread in the world, present yet a further challenge in upholding the Bahá'í standard of conduct with respect to financial affairs. Nevertheless, following in the footsteps of your spiritual forebears, you remain undaunted, striving sincerely to reinforce within your families, particularly in your children, attitudes towards material wealth founded on Divine guidance. The members of the younger generation would do well to ponder the above statement of 'Abdu'l-Bahá in which He conditions the acquisition of wealth on diligent work and the grace of God. Let them weigh carefully in their hearts and minds the difference between gaining wealth through earnest effort in fields such as agriculture, commerce, the arts, and industry, on the one hand, and, on the other, obtaining it without exertion or through dishonourable means. Let them consider the consequences of each for the spiritual development of the individual, as well as the progress of society, and ask themselves what possibilities exist for generating income and acquiring wealth that will draw down confirmations from on high. It will surely become evident, as they do so, that what will attract God's blessings and ensure true happiness both in this world and in the next is the development of spiritual qualities, such as honesty, trustworthiness, generosity, justice, and consideration for others, and the recognition that material means are to be expended for the betterment of the world.

Many would readily acknowledge that the acquisition of wealth should be governed by the requirements of justice, which, as a principle, can be expressed to varying degrees, on different levels. An employer and employee, for example, are bound by the laws and conventions that regulate their work, and each is expected to carry out his or her responsibilities with honesty and integrity. At another level, however, if the deeper implications of justice are to be realized, the other two preconditions to the legitimate acquisition of wealth mentioned above must be taken into account, and prevailing norms reassessed in their light. Here, the relationship between minimum wage and the cost of living merits careful evaluation—this, especially in light of the contribution workers make to a company's success and their entitlement, as noted by 'Abdu'l-Bahá, to a fair share of the profits. The wide margin, often unjustifiable, between the production costs of certain goods and the price at which they are sold likewise requires attention, as does the question of the generation of wealth through measures that "enrich the generality of the people." What such reflection and inquiry will no doubt make abundantly clear is that certain approaches to obtaining wealth—so many of which involve the exploitation of others, the monopolization and manipulation of markets, and the production of goods that promote violence and immorality—are unworthy and unacceptable.

Today the world is assailed by an array of destructive forces. Materialism, rooted in the West, has now spread to every corner of the planet, breeding, in the name of a strong global economy and human welfare, a culture of consumerism. It skilfully and ingeniously promotes a habit of consumption that seeks to satisfy the basest and most selfish desires, while encouraging the expenditure of wealth so as to prolong and exacerbate social conflict. How vain and foolish a worldview! And meanwhile, a rising tide of fundamentalism, bringing with it an exceedingly narrow understanding of religion and spirituality, continues to gather strength, threatening to engulf humanity in rigid dogmatism. In its most extreme form, it conditions the resolution of the problems of the world upon the occurrence of events derived from illogical and superstitious notions. It professes to uphold virtue yet, in practice, perpetuates oppression and greed. Among the deplorable results of the operation of such forces are a deepening confusion on the part of young people everywhere, a sense of hopelessness in the ranks of those who would drive progress, and the emergence of a myriad social maladies.

The key to resolving these social ills rests in the hands of a youthful generation convinced of the nobility of human beings; eagerly seeking a deeper understanding of the true purpose of existence; able to distinguish between divine religion and mere superstition; clear in the view of science and religion as two independent yet complementary systems of knowledge that propel human progress; conscious of and drawn to the beauty and power of unity in diversity; secure in the knowledge that real glory is to be found in service to one's country and to the peoples of the world; and mindful that the acquisition of wealth is praiseworthy only insofar as it is attained through just means and expended for benevolent purposes, for the promotion of knowledge and toward the common good. Thus must our precious youth prepare themselves to shoulder the tremendous responsibilities that await them. And thus will they prove immune to the atmosphere of greed that surrounds them and press forward unwavering in the pursuit of their exalted goals. (The Universal House of Justice, letter dated 2 April 2010, to the Believers in the Cradle of the Faith)

Your comments concerning poverty emphasize the extent to which society must change its attitudes before a solution to that social problem can be found. It is not simply a matter of economics; the solution deeply involves the adoption of spiritual principles at the grassroots as well as among governments. (From a letter written on behalf of the Universal House of Justice, dated 27 April 1988, to an individual believer)

Since the body of humankind is one and indivisible, each member of the race is born into the world as a trust of the whole. This trusteeship constitutes the moral foundation of most of the other rights—principally economic and social—which the instruments of the United Nations are attempting similarly to define. The security of the family and the home, the ownership of property, and the right to privacy are all implied in such a trusteeship. The obligations on the part of the community extend to the provision of employment, mental and physical health care, social security, fair wages, rest and recreation, and a host of other reasonable expectations on the part of the individual members of society. (Bahá'í International Community, *The Prosperity of Humankind*)

The contemporary realization of humanity's collective oneness comes after a historic process in which individuals were fused into ever greater units. Moving from clans, to tribes, to city-states, to nations, the next inevitable step for humanity is nothing less than the creation of a global civilization. In this new global civilization, all people and peoples are component parts of a single great organism—an organism that is human civilization itself. As stated by Bahá'u'lláh more than 100 years ago, "The earth is but one country, and mankind its citizens."

Further, as explained in the Bahá'í writings, the oneness of humanity "implies an organic change in the structure of present-day society, a change such as the world has not yet experienced. . . . It calls for no less than the reconstruction and the demilitarization of the whole civilized world—a world organically unified in all the essential aspects of its life, its political machinery, its spiritual aspiration, its trade and finance, its script and language, and yet infinite in the diversity of the national characteristics of its federated units."

In considering the themes of the World Conference against Racism, a proper understanding of the reality of the oneness of humanity holds a number of implications.

It implies that any law, tradition or mental construct that grants superior rights or privileges to one grouping of humanity over another is not only morally wrong but fundamentally at odds with the best interests of even those who consider themselves to be in some way superior. It implies that nation-states, as the building blocks of a global civilization, must hold to common standards of rights and take active steps to purge from their laws, traditions and practices any form of discrimination based on race, nationality or ethnic origin.

It implies that justice must be the ruling principle of social organization, a corollary principle that calls for widespread measures on the part of governments, their agencies, and civil society to address economic injustice at all levels. The Bahá'í writings call for both voluntary giving and government measures, such as the "equalization and apportionment" of excess wealth, so that the great disparities between the rich and the poor are eliminated. The Bahá'í writings also prescribe specific measures, such as profit-sharing and the equation of work with worship, that promote general economic prosperity across all classes. (Bahá'í International Community, 31 August 2001, "Statement to World Conference against Racism")

The Bahá'í approach to the problem of extreme poverty is based on the belief that economic problems can be solved only through the application of spiritual principles. This approach suggests that to adjust the economic relationships of society, man's character must first be transformed. Until the actions of humankind promote justice above the satisfaction of greed and readjusts the world's economies accordingly, the gap between the rich and the poor will continue to widen, and the dream of sustainable economic growth, peace, and prosperity must remain elusive. Sensitizing mankind to the vital role of spirituality in solving economic problems including the realization of universal equitable access to wealth and opportunity will, we are convinced, create a new impetus for change.

A new economic order can be founded only on an unshakable conviction of the oneness of mankind. Discussions aimed at solving problems related to extreme poverty based on the premise that we are one human family rapidly expand beyond the current vocabulary of economics. They demand a wider context, one which anticipates the emergence of a global system of relationships resting on the principles of equity and justice. . . .

The Bahá'í writings anticipate the development of communities in which the well-being of every member is the concern of the community as a whole. The centre of such a community would include social service institutions which shall afford relief to the suffering, sustenance to the poor, shelter to the wayfarer, solace to the bereaved, and education to the ignorant.

In the New World Order envisaged by Bahá'u'lláh, rights are inseparable from responsibilities. A fundamental purpose of life is to contribute to the advancement of civilization. Idleness and begging are unacceptable in a well-functioning society, while work performed in the spirit of service is elevated to the station of worship. Thus the right to work, the right to contribute to society, takes on a spiritual dimension, and the responsibility to be productive applies to everyone. (Bahá'í International Community, Statement to the 49th Session of the United Nations Commission on Human Rights, 12 February 1993, "Human Rights and Extreme Poverty")

Capital and Labor, Private Ownership

The Teachings do not state what the exact relationship between Labour and Capital will be in the future. Neither do they indicate any directions regarding the payment of wages, or whether the wage system will be retained, modified or altogether abolished. They, however, explicitly uphold the institution of private ownership, but stress also the necessity of introducing certain fundamental changes in its methods and features. (From a letter written on behalf of Shoghi Effendi, dated 22 April 1939, to an individual believer, in "Wealth: Redistribution of")

Regarding your questions concerning the Bahá'í attitude on various economic problems, such as the problem of ownership, control and distribution of capital, and of other means of production, the problem of trusts and monopolies, and such economic experiments as social cooperatives; the Teachings of Bahá'u'lláh and 'Abdu'l-Bahá do not provide specific and detailed solutions to all such economic questions which mostly pertain to the domain of technical economics, and as such do not concern directly the

Cause. True, there are certain guiding principles in Bahá'í Sacred Writings on the subject of economics, but these do by no means cover the whole field of theoretical and applied economics, and are mostly intended to guide further Bahá'í economic writers and technicians to evolve an economic system which would function in full conformity with the spirit and the exact provisions of the Cause on this and similar subjects. The International House of Justice will have, in consultation with economic experts, to assist in the formulation and evolution of the Bahá'í economic system of the future. One thing, however, is certain that the Cause neither accepts the theories of the Capitalistic economics in full, nor can it agree with the Marxists and Communists in their repudiation of the principle of private ownership and of the vital sacred rights of the individual. (From a letter written on behalf of Shoghi Effendi, dated 10 June 1930, to an individual believer, in *Lights of Guidance,* no. 1862)

The ideologies now current in the world are extremely complex. Just as it is difficult to identify any longer a coherent system of teachings which could be called Christianity and embrace all those who call themselves Christians, so there are many kinds of Communist, often stridently at variance with one another. Even more so are there many kinds of "Capitalist" in the sense of those who advocate Capitalism as the most desirable form of economic system. . . .

One could postulate two extremes of economic theory: those who believe that the best solution is to remove all governmental control and intervention from the operation of the economic system, and those who believe that the functioning of the economic system should be closely supervised and adjusted by the State so that society is not at the mercy of the system but has it under its control. As has become abundantly clear, neither extreme is workable, and proponents of both have gradually come to adopt more moderate stances, although there tends to be an oscillation of viewpoints in response to changing conditions. It was to the proponents of one of these extremes and to the current highly unsatisfactory economic situation in the

world that the House of Justice was alluding when it referred to those ideologies which have tended "to callously abandon starving millions to the
operations of a market system that all too clearly is aggravating the plight of
the majority of mankind, while enabling small sections to live in a condition
of affluence scarcely dreamed of by our forebears." (The Universal House
of Justice, letter dated 13 November 1985, in "Economics, Agriculture, and
Related Subjects")

Generosity and Voluntary Sharing

O Son of Man! Bestow My wealth upon My poor, that in heaven thou
mayest draw from stores of unfading splendor and treasures of imperishable
glory. (Bahá'u'lláh, The Hidden Words, Arabic, no. 57)

Say: The appointed Day is come. This is the Springtime of benevolent deeds,
were ye of them that comprehend. Strive ye with all your might, O people,
that ye may bring forth that which will truly profit you in the worlds of your
Lord, the All-Glorious, the All-Praised. (Bahá'u'lláh, in *The Compilation of
Compilations*, vol. I, no. 1123)

The fourth Taraz concerneth trustworthiness. Verily it is the door of security for all that dwell on earth and a token of glory on the part of the All-
Merciful. He who partaketh thereof hath indeed partaken of the treasures
of wealth and prosperity. Trustworthiness is the greatest portal leading unto
the tranquility and security of the people. In truth the stability of every
affair hath depended and doth depend upon it. All the domains of power,
of grandeur and of wealth are illumined by its light. (Bahá'u'lláh, *Tablets of
Bahá'u'lláh*, p. 37)

Commerce is as a heaven, whose sun is trustworthiness and whose moon is
truthfulness. (Bahá'u'lláh, in *The Compilation of Compilations*, vol. II, no.
2058)

Service to the friends is service to the Kingdom of God, and consideration shown to the poor is one of the greatest teachings of God. ('Abdu'l-Bahá, *Selections from the Writings of 'Abdu'l-Bahá*, no. 11.1)

Should a wealthy man choose to bequeath, upon his death, a portion of his wealth to the poor and needy, perchance this action will bring about divine pardon and forgiveness and result in his progress in the Kingdom of the All-Merciful. ('Abdu'l-Bahá, *Some Answered Questions*, no. 62.5)

Those souls who are of the Kingdom eagerly wish to be of service to the poor, to sympathize with them, to show kindness to the miserable and to make their lives fruitful. Happy art thou that thou hast such a wish. ('Abdu'l-Bahá, *Selections from the Writings of 'Abdu'l-Bahá*, no. 80.1)

To state the matter briefly, the Teachings of Bahá'u'lláh advocate voluntary sharing, and this is a greater thing than the equalization of wealth. For equalization must be imposed from without, while sharing is a matter of free choice.

Man reacheth perfection through good deeds, voluntarily performed, not through good deeds the doing of which was forced upon him. And sharing is a personally chosen righteous act: that is, the rich should extend assistance to the poor, they should expend their substance for the poor, but of their own free will, and not because the poor have gained this end by force. For the harvest of force is turmoil and the ruin of the social order. On the other hand voluntary sharing, the freely-chosen expending of one's substance, leadeth to society's comfort and peace. It lighteth up the world; it bestoweth honor upon humankind. ('Abdu'l-Bahá, *Selections from the Writings of 'Abdu'l-Bahá*, no. 79.2–3)

And among the teachings of Bahá'u'lláh is voluntary sharing of one's property with others among mankind. This voluntary sharing is greater than equality, and consists in this, that man should not prefer himself to others, but rather should sacrifice his life and property for others. But this should not be introduced by coercion so that it becomes a law and man is compelled to follow it. Nay, rather, man should voluntarily and of his own choice sacrifice his property and life for others, and spend willingly for the poor, just as is done in Persia among the Bahá'ís. ('Abdu'l-Bahá, *Selections from the Writings of 'Abdu'l-Bahá*, no. 227.19)

Hearts must be so cemented together, love must become so dominant that the rich shall most willingly extend assistance to the poor and take steps to establish these economic adjustments permanently. If it is accomplished in this way, it will be most praiseworthy because then it will be for the sake of God and in the pathway of His service. For example, it will be as if the rich inhabitants of a city should say, "It is neither just nor lawful that we should possess great wealth while there is abject poverty in this community," and then willingly give their wealth to the poor, retaining only as much as will enable them to live comfortably. ('Abdu'l-Bahá, *The Promulgation of Universal Peace,* pp. 334)

We must be like the fountain or spring that is continually emptying itself of all that it has and is continually being refilled from an invisible source. To be continually giving out for the good of our fellows undeterred by the fear of poverty and reliant on the unfailing bounty of the Source of all wealth and all good—this is the secret of right living. (Shoghi Effendi, *Principles of Bahá'í Administration,* p. 20)

A large share of the responsibility for poverty eradication rests with the individuals themselves. While poverty is the product of numerous factors: historic, economic, political and environmental, there is also a cultural dimension, which manifests itself in individual values and attitudes. Some of these—such as the subjugation of girls and women, the lack of value of education or of an individual's right to progress—can exacerbate conditions of poverty. The relevant human qualities such as honesty, willingness to work, and cooperation can be harnessed to accomplish enormously demanding goals when members of society trust that they are protected by standards of justice and assured of benefits that apply equally to all. The human rights approach, with its emphasis on the individual's entitlement to a set of rights, however, may prove challenging to implement without an accompanying moral influence necessary to inspire the accompanying changes in attitudes and behaviors. (Bahá'í International Community, Statement to the 49th Session of the United Nations Commission on Human Rights, February 12, 1993, "Human Rights and Extreme Poverty")

Legislative and Tax Systems

Bahá'u'lláh has given instructions regarding every one of the questions confronting humanity. He has given teachings and instructions with regard to every one of the problems with which man struggles. Among them are [the teachings] concerning the question of economics, that all the members of the body politic may enjoy through the working out of this solution the greatest happiness, welfare and comfort without any harm or injury attacking the general order of things. Thereby no difference or dissension will occur. No sedition or contention will take place. This solution is this:

First and foremost is the principle that to all the members of the body politic shall be given the greatest achievements of the world of humanity. Each one shall have the utmost welfare and well-being. To solve this problem we must begin with the farmer; there will we lay a foundation for system and order because the peasant class and the agricultural class exceed other classes in the importance of their service. In every village there must be established a general storehouse which will have a number of revenues.

The first revenue will be that of the tenth or tithes.

The second revenue [will be derived] from the animals.

The third revenue, from the minerals; that is to say, every mine prospected or discovered, a third thereof will go to this vast storehouse.

The fourth is this: whosoever dies without leaving any heirs, all his heritage will go to the general storehouse.

Fifth, if any treasures shall be found on the land, they should be devoted to this storehouse.

All these revenues will be assembled in this storehouse.

As to the first, the tenths or tithes: We will consider a farmer, . . . We will look into his income. We will find out for instance, what is his annual revenue and also what are his expenditures. Now, if his income be equal to his expenditures, from such a farmer nothing whatever will be taken. That is, he will not be subjected to taxation of any sort, needing as he does all his income. Another farmer may have expenses running up to one thousand dollars, we will say, and his income is two thousand dollars. From such an one a tenth will be required, because he has a surplus. But if his income be ten thousand dollars and his expenses one thousand dollars or his income twenty thousand dollars, he will have to pay as taxes, one fourth. If his income be one hundred thousand dollars, and his expenses five thousand, one third will he have to pay because he has still a surplus since his expenses are five thousand and his income one hundred thousand. If he pays, say, thirty-five thousand dollars, in addition to the expenditure of five thousand he still has sixty thousand left. But if his expenses be ten thousand and his income two hundred thousand, then he must give an even half because ninety thousand will be in that case the sum remaining. Such a scale as this will determine allotment of taxes. All the income from such revenues will go to this general storehouse.

Then there must be considered such emergencies as follows: A certain farmer whose expenses run up to ten thousand dollars and whose income is only five thousand will receive necessary expenses from the storehouse. Five thousand dollars will be allotted to him so he will not be in need.

Then the orphans will be looked after, all of whose expenses will be taken care of. The cripples in the village—all their expenses will be looked after. The poor in the village—their necessary expenses will be defrayed. And other members who for valid reasons are incapacitated—the blind, the old, the deaf—their comfort must be looked after. In the village no one will remain in need or in want. All will live in the utmost comfort and welfare. Yet no schism will assail the general order of the body politic.

Hence, the expenses or expenditures of the general storehouse are now made clear and its activities made manifest. The income of this general storehouse has been shown. Certain trustees will be elected by the people in a given village to look after these transactions. The farmers will be taken care of, and, if after all these expenses are defrayed, any surplus is found in the storehouse, it must be transferred to the national treasury.

This system is all thus ordered so that in the village the very poor will be comfortable, the orphans will live happily and well; in a word, no one will be left destitute. All the individual members of the body politic will thus live comfortably and well.

For larger cities, naturally, there will be a system on a larger scale. Were I to go into that solution the details thereof would be very lengthy.

The result of this [system] will be that each individual member of the body politic will live most comfortably and happily under obligation to no one. . . . ('Abdu'l-Bahá, *The Promulgation of Universal Peace*, pp. 438–39)

The essence of the Bahá'í spirit is that, in order to establish a better social order and economic condition, there must be allegiance to the laws and principles of government. Under the laws which are to govern the world, the socialists may justly demand human rights but without resort to force and violence. The governments will enact these laws, establishing just legislation and economics in order that all humanity may enjoy a full measure of welfare and privilege; but this will always be according to legal protection and procedure. Without legislative administration, rights and demands fail, and the welfare of the commonwealth cannot be realized. Today the method of demand is the strike and resort to force, which is manifestly wrong and destructive of human foundations. Rightful privilege and demand must be set forth in laws and regulations. ('Abdu'l-Bahá, *The Promulgation of Universal Peace*, pp. 333–34)

Although it will resemble the present system in many ways, the evolving economic system which Bahá'ís envision will have significant points of distinction.

Let us take as an example the Bahá'í view of income distribution, which allows for differences but would eliminate both extreme wealth and extreme poverty. The accumulation of excessive fortunes by a small number of individuals, while the masses are in need, is, according to Bahá'í teachings, an iniquity and an injustice. Moderation should, therefore, be established by means of laws and regulations that would hinder the accumulation of excessive fortunes by a few individuals and provide for the essential needs of the masses. (Bahá'í International Community, 12 February 1993, "Human Rights and Extreme Poverty")

Absolute Equality is Untenable

Bahá'u'lláh taught that an equal standard of human rights must be recognized and adopted. In the estimation of God all men are equal; there is no distinction or preferment for any soul in the dominion of His justice and equity. ('Abdu'l-Bahá, *The Promulgation of Universal Peace*, p. 252)

The arrangements of the circumstances of the people must be such that poverty shall disappear, that everyone, as far as possible, according to his rank and position, shall share in comfort and well-being.

We see amongst us men who are overburdened with riches on the one hand, and on the other those unfortunate ones who starve with nothing; those who possess several stately palaces, and those who have not where to lay their head. Some we find with numerous courses of costly and dainty food; whilst others can scarce find sufficient crusts to keep them alive. Whilst some are clothed in velvets, furs and fine linen, others have insufficient, poor and thin garments with which to protect them from the cold.

This condition of affairs is wrong, and must be remedied. Now the remedy must be carefully undertaken. It cannot be done by bringing to pass absolute equality between men.

Equality is a chimera! It is entirely impracticable! Even if equality could be achieved it could not continue—and if its existence were possible, the whole order of the world would be destroyed. The law of order must always obtain in the world of humanity. Heaven has so decreed in the creation of man.

Some are full of intelligence, others have an ordinary amount of it, and others again are devoid of intellect. In these three classes of men there is order but not equality. How could it be possible that wisdom and stupidity should be equal? Humanity, like a great army, requires a general, captains, under-officers in their degree, and soldiers, each with their own appointed duties. Degrees are absolutely necessary to ensure an orderly organization. An army could not be composed of generals alone, or of captains only, or of nothing but soldiers without one in authority. The certain result of such a plan would be that disorder and demoralization would overtake the whole army.

King Lycurgus, the philosopher, made a great plan to equalize the subjects of Sparta; with self-sacrifice and wisdom was the experiment begun. Then the king called the people of his kingdom, and made them swear a great oath to maintain the same order of government if he should leave the country, also that nothing should make them alter it until his return. Having secured this oath, he left his kingdom of Sparta and never returned. Lycurgus abandoned the situation, renouncing his high position, thinking to achieve the permanent good of his country by the equalization of the property and of the conditions of life in his kingdom. All the self-sacrifice of the king was in vain. The great experiment failed. After a time all was destroyed; his carefully thought-out constitution came to an end.

The futility of attempting such a scheme was shown and the impossibility of attaining equal conditions of existence was proclaimed in the ancient kingdom of Sparta. In our day any such attempt would be equally doomed to failure. ('Abdu'l-Bahá, *Paris Talks*, no. 46.3–9)

Difference of capacity in human individuals is fundamental. It is impossible for all to be alike, all to be equal, all to be wise. Bahá'u'lláh has revealed principles and laws which will accomplish the adjustment of varying human capacities. He has said that whatsoever is possible of accomplishment in human government will be effected through these principles. When the laws He has instituted are carried out, there will be no millionaires possible in the community and likewise no extremely poor. ('Abdu'l-Bahá, *The Promulgation of Universal Peace*, p. 303)

As to the innate character, although the innate nature bestowed by God upon man is purely good, yet that character differs among men according to the degrees they occupy: All degrees are good, but some are more so than others. Thus every human being possesses intelligence and capacity, but intelligence, capacity, and aptitude differ from person to person. This is self-evident.

For example, take a number of children from the same place and family, attending the same school and instructed by the same teacher, raised on the same food and in the same climate, wearing the same clothing and studying the same lessons: It is certain that among these children some will become skilled in the arts and sciences, some will be of average ability, and some will be dull. It is therefore clear that in man's innate nature there is a difference in degree, aptitude, and capacity, but it is not a matter of good or evil—it is merely a difference of degree. ('Abdu'l-Bahá, *Some Answered Questions*, no. 57.3–4)

One of Bahá'u'lláh's teachings is the adjustment of means of livelihood in human society. Under this adjustment there can be no extremes in human conditions as regards wealth and sustenance. For the community needs financier, farmer, merchant and laborer just as an army must be composed of commander, officers and privates. All cannot be commanders; all cannot be officers or privates. Each in his station in the social fabric must be competent—each in his function according to ability but with justness of opportunity for all. ('Abdu'l-Bahá, *The Promulgation of Universal Peace*, pp. 301–2)

The body politic may well be likened to an army. In this army there must be a general, there must be a sergeant, there must be a marshal, there must be the infantry; but all must enjoy the greatest comfort and welfare.

83

God is not partial and is no respecter of persons. He has made provision for all. The harvest comes forth for everyone. The rain showers upon everybody and the heat of the sun is destined to warm everyone. The verdure of the earth is for everyone. Therefore, there should be for all humanity the utmost happiness, the utmost comfort, the utmost well-being. ('Abdu'l-Bahá, *The Promulgation of Universal Peace,* p. 439)

The Master has definitely stated that wages should be unequal, simply because that men are unequal in their ability and hence should receive wages that would correspond to their varying capacities and resources. (Shoghi Effendi, *Directives from the Guardian,* p. 20)

Social inequality is the inevitable outcome of the natural inequality of men. Human beings are different in ability and should, therefore, be different in their social and economic standing. Extremes of wealth and poverty should, however, be totally abolished. Those whose brains have contributed to the creation and improvement of the means of production must be fairly rewarded, though these means may be owned and controlled by others. (From a letter written on behalf of Shoghi Effendi, dated 26 January 1935, to an individual believer, in *Lights of Guidance,* no. 1865)

An equal standard of human rights must be upheld, and individuals given equal opportunities. Variety and not uniformity is the principle of organic society. Since lack of opportunity, repression and degrading conditions have created masses of people unable to exercise the functions of citizenship, such persons are a moral trust laid upon the conscience of the rest, to educate the ignorant, train the immature and heal the sick.

The human person is the spiritual entity of mankind, but the family is the inviolable and divinely created social entity. The right of the individual to survive is identified with the right of the family to maintain itself under conditions favorable to body, mind and spirit. While the mature individual is the political unit, the family constitutes the economic unit, and income operates on the basis of family living and welfare. (Bahá'í International Community, *A Bahá'í Declaration of Human Obligations and Rights*)

Benevolent Use of Corporate Wealth
Economic considerations underlying poverty alleviation efforts have generally focused on the creation of wealth but have not yet fully considered the parallel problem of the over-concentration of wealth. In an interconnected world, where the wealth of many of the world's richest individuals exceeds the Gross Domestic Product of entire nations, extreme poverty and extreme wealth exist side by side. While much of the focus of remedial efforts is directed towards the poorest, it is the concentration of wealth in the hands of the few that is in urgent need of attention. Indeed, the tremendous wealth generated by transnational corporations could be an integral part of the solution to tackle poverty, through strict regulation to ensure good global citizenship, adherence to human rights norms and the distribution of wealth for the benefit of the larger society. Where a nation's wealth is concerned, the question becomes one of social value rather than gross dollar measures. The Gross Domestic Product, for example, aggregates the sum total of all economic activity—including the production of guns, cigarettes, etc.—regardless of its social worth or environmental impact. New measures that account for pollutants and economic ills and add unmeasured, unremunerated benefits are needed for a more accurate picture of a nation's economic health and wealth. (Bahá'í International Community, "Eradicating Poverty: Moving Forward as One")

Strikes, Profit Sharing, Legal Protections
You have asked about strikes. Great difficulties have arisen and will continue to arise from this issue. The origin of these difficulties is twofold: One is the excessive greed and rapacity of the factory owners, and the other is the gratuitous demands, the greed, and the intransigence of the workers. One must therefore seek to address both.

Now, the root cause of these difficulties lies in the law of nature that governs present-day civilization, for it results in a handful of people accumulating vast fortunes that far exceed their needs, while the greater number remain naked, destitute, and helpless. This is at once contrary to justice, to humanity, and to fairness; it is the very height of inequity and runs counter to the good-pleasure of the All-Merciful.

This disparity is confined to the human race: Among other creatures, that is, among the animals, a certain kind of justice and equality prevails. Thus there is equality within a shepherd's flock, or within a herd of deer in the wilderness, or among the songbirds that dwell in the mountains, plains, and orchards. The animals of every species enjoy a measure of equality and do not differ greatly from one another in their means of existence, and thus they live in perfect peace and joy.

It is quite otherwise with the human race, where the greatest oppression and injustice are to be found. Thus you can observe, on the one hand, a single person who has amassed a fortune, made an entire country his personal dominion, acquired immense wealth, and secured an unceasing flow of gains and profits, and, on the other, a hundred thousand helpless souls—weak, powerless, and wanting even a mouthful of bread. There is neither equality here nor benevolence. Observe how, as a result, general peace and happiness have become so wanting, and the welfare of humanity so undermined, that the lives of a vast multitude have been rendered fruitless! For all the wealth, power, commerce, and industry are concentrated in the hands of a few individuals, while all others toil under the burden of endless hardships and difficulties, are bereft of advantages and benefits, and remain deprived of comfort and peace. One must therefore enact such laws and regulations as will moderate the excessive fortunes of the few and meet the basic needs of the myriad millions of the poor, that a degree of moderation may be achieved.

However, absolute equality is just as untenable, for complete equality in wealth, power, commerce, agriculture, and industry would result in chaos and disorder, disrupt livelihoods, provoke universal discontent, and undermine the orderly conduct of the affairs of the community. For unjustified equality is also fraught with peril. It is preferable, then, that some measure of moderation be achieved, and by moderation is meant the enactment of such laws and regulations as would prevent the unwarranted concentration of wealth in the hands of the few and satisfy the essential needs of the many. For instance, the factory owners reap a fortune every day, but the wage the poor workers are paid cannot even meet their daily needs: This is most unfair, and assuredly no just man can accept it. Therefore, laws and regulations should be enacted which would grant the workers both a daily wage and a share in a fourth or fifth of the profits of the factory in accordance with its means, or which would have the workers equitably share in some other way in the profits with the owners. For the capital and the management come from the latter and the toil and labour from the former. The workers could either be granted a wage that adequately meets their daily needs, as well as a right to a share in the revenues of the factory when they are injured, incapacitated, or unable to work, or else a wage could be set that allows the workers to both satisfy their daily needs and save a little for times of weakness and incapacity.

If matters were so arranged, neither would the factory owners amass each day a fortune which is absolutely of no use to them—for should one's fortune increase beyond measure, one would come under a most heavy burden, become subject to exceeding hardships and troubles, and find the administration of such an excessive fortune to be most difficult and to exhaust one's natural powers—nor would the workers endure such toil and hardship as to become incapacitated and to fall victim, at the end of their lives, to the direst need.

It is therefore clearly established that the appropriation of excessive wealth by a few individuals, notwithstanding the needs of the masses, is unfair and unjust, and that, conversely, absolute equality would also disrupt the existence, welfare, comfort, peace, and orderly life of the human race. Such being the case, the best course is therefore to seek moderation, which is for the wealthy to recognize the advantages of moderation in the acquisition of profits and to show regard for the welfare of the poor and the needy, that is, to fix a daily wage for the workers and also to allot them a share of the total profits of the factory.

In brief, insofar as the mutual rights of the factory owners and the workers are concerned, laws must be enacted that would enable the former to make reasonable profits and the latter to be provided with their present necessities and their future needs, so that if they become incapacitated, grow old, or die and leave behind small children, they or their children will not be overcome by dire poverty but will receive a modest pension from the revenues of the factory itself.

For their part, the workers should not make excessive demands, be recalcitrant, ask for more than they deserve, or go on strike. They should obey and comply and make no demands for exorbitant wages. Rather, the mutual and equitable rights of both parties should be officially fixed and established according to the laws of justice and compassion, and any party that violates them should be condemned after a fair hearing and be subject to a definitive verdict enforced by the executive branch, so that all affairs may be appropriately ordered and all problems adequately resolved.

The intervention of the government and the courts in the problems arising between owners and workers is fully warranted, since these are not such particular matters as are ordinary transactions between two individuals, which do not concern the public and in which the government should have no right to interfere. For problems between owners and workers, though they may appear to be a private matter, are detrimental to the common good, since the commercial, industrial, and agricultural affairs, and even the general business of the nation, are all intimately linked together: An impairment to one is a loss to all. And since the problems between owners and workers are detrimental to the common good, the government and the courts have therefore the right to intervene.

Even in the case of differences that arise between two individuals with regard to particular rights, a third party, namely the government, is needed to resolve the dispute. How, then, can the problem of strikes, which entirely disrupt the country—whether they arise from the inordinate demands of the workers or the excessive greed of the factory owners—remain neglected?

Gracious God! How can one see one's fellow men hungry, destitute, and deprived, and yet live in peace and comfort in one's splendid mansion? How can one see others in the greatest need and yet take delight in one's fortune? That is why it has been decreed in the divine religions that the wealthy should offer up each year a portion of their wealth for the sustenance of the poor and the assistance of the needy. This is one of the foundations of the religion of God and is an injunction binding upon all. And since in this regard one is not outwardly compelled or obliged by the government, but rather aids the poor at the prompting of one's own heart and in a spirit of joy and radiance, such a deed is most commendable, approved, and pleasing. ('Abdu'l-Bahá, *Some Answered Questions,* no. 78.1–12)

. . . Bahá'u'lláh did not bring a complete system of economics to the world. Profit sharing is recommended as a solution to one form of economic problems. There is nothing in the teachings against some kind of capitalism; its present form, though, would require adjustments to be made.

There are practically no technical teachings on economics in the Cause, such as banking, the price system, and others. (Shoghi Effendi, *Directives from the Guardian,* p. 20)

With regard to your question concerning the Bahá'í attitude towards labour problems; these cannot assuredly be solved, . . . through the sheer force of physical violence. Non-cooperation too, even though not accompanied by acts of violence, is ineffective. The conflict between labour and capital can best be solved through the peaceful and constructive methods of cooperation and of consultation.

The Bahá'ís, therefore, are advised to avoid, as much as they can, getting mixed in labour strikes and trouble, and particularly to desist from all acts of physical violence which indeed run counter to the very spirit of the Cause. The Faith of Bahá'u'lláh stands for peace, harmony, and cooperation between the individuals and nations of the world. (From a letter written on behalf of the Universal House of Justice, dated 4 April 1973, to the National Spiritual Assembly of Luxembourg, in *Lights of Guidance,* no. 1404)

Education for Prosperity

The primary, the most urgent requirement is the promotion of education. It is inconceivable that any nation should achieve prosperity and success unless this paramount, this fundamental concern is carried forward. The principal reason for the decline and fall of peoples is ignorance. Today the mass of the people are uninformed even as to ordinary affairs, how much less do they grasp the core of the important problems and complex needs of the time. ('Abdu'l-Bahá, *The Secret of Divine Civilization,* ¶193)

Observe carefully how education and the arts of civilization bring honor, prosperity, independence and freedom to a government and its people. ('Abdu'l-Bahá, *The Secret of Divine Civilization,* ¶196)

Now observe that it is education that brings East and West under man's dominion, produces all these marvellous crafts, promotes these mighty arts and sciences, and gives rise to these new discoveries and undertakings. Were it not for an educator, the means of comfort, civilization, and human virtues could in no wise have been acquired. If a man is left alone in a wilderness where he sees none of his own kind, he will undoubtedly become a mere animal. It is therefore clear that an educator is needed.

But education is of three kinds: material, human, and spiritual. Material education aims at the growth and development of the body, and consists in securing its sustenance and obtaining the means of its ease and comfort. This education is common to both man and animal.

Human education, however, consists in civilization and progress, that is, sound governance, social order, human welfare, commerce and industry, arts and sciences, momentous discoveries, and great undertakings, which are the central features distinguishing man from the animal.

As to divine education, it is the education of the Kingdom and consists in acquiring divine perfections. This is indeed true education, for by its virtue man becomes the focal centre of divine blessings and the embodiment of the verse "Let Us make man in Our image, after Our likeness."* This is the ultimate goal of the world of humanity. ('Abdu'l-Bahá, *Some Answered Questions*, no. 3.4–7)

It is in the context of raising the level of human capacity through the expansion of knowledge at all levels that the economic issues facing humankind need to be addressed. As the experience of recent decades has demonstrated, material benefits and endeavors cannot be regarded as ends in themselves. Their value consists not only in providing for humanity's basic needs in housing, food, health care, and the like, but in extending the reach of human abilities. The most important role that economic efforts must play in development lies, therefore, in equipping people and institutions with the means through which they can achieve the real purpose of development: that is, laying foundations for a new social order that can cultivate the limitless potentialities latent in human consciousness. (Bahá'í International Community, *The Prosperity of Humankind*)

Economic Policies for an Interdependent World
And among the teachings of Bahá'u'lláh is that religious, racial, political, economic and patriotic prejudices destroy the edifice of humanity. As long as these prejudices prevail, the world of humanity will not have rest. For a period of 6,000 years history informs us about the world of humanity. During these 6,000 years the world of humanity has not been free from war, strife, murder and bloodthirstiness. . . .

Regarding the economic prejudice, it is apparent that whenever the ties between nations become strengthened and the exchange of commodities accelerated, and any economic principle is established in one country, it will

---

* Genesis 1:26.

ultimately affect the other countries and universal benefits will result. Then why this prejudice? ('Abdu'l-Bahá, *Selections from the Writings of 'Abdu'l-Bahá,* no. 227.11, 15)

In like manner all the members of the human family, whether peoples or governments, cities or villages, have become increasingly interdependent. For none is self-sufficiency any longer possible, inasmuch as political ties unite all peoples and nations, and the bonds of trade and industry, of agriculture and education, are being strengthened every day. Hence the unity of all mankind can in this day be achieved. ('Abdu'l-Bahá, *Selections from the Writings of 'Abdu'l-Bahá,* no. 15.6)

The world is, in truth, moving on towards its destiny. The interdependence of the peoples and nations of the earth, whatever the leaders of the divisive forces of the world may say or do, is already an accomplished fact. Its unity in the economic sphere is now understood and recognized. The welfare of the part means the welfare of the whole, and the distress of the part brings distress to the whole. (Shoghi Effendi, *The Promised Day Is Come,* ¶300)

No country can possibly solve its economic difficulties alone, for economic interdependence is an unescapable economic reality, a fact of economic life which can neither be ignored nor deliberately opposed. (From a letter written on behalf of Shoghi Effendi, dated 22 April 1939, to an individual believer, in *"Wealth: Redistribution of"*)

A world community in which all economic barriers will have been permanently demolished and the interdependence of Capital and Labor definitely recognized; in which the clamor of religious fanaticism and strife will have been forever stilled; in which the flame of racial animosity will have been finally extinguished; in which a single code of international law—the product of the considered judgment of the world's federated representatives—shall have as its sanction the instant and coercive intervention of the combined forces of the federated units; and finally a world community in which the fury of a capricious and militant nationalism will have been transmuted into an abiding consciousness of world citizenship—such indeed, appears, in its broadest outline, the Order anticipated by Bahá'u'lláh, an Order that shall come to be regarded as the fairest fruit of a slowly maturing age. (Shoghi Effendi, *The World Order of Bahá'u'lláh*, p. 41)

Those who care for the future of the human race may well ponder this advice. If long-cherished ideals and time-honored institutions, if certain social assumptions and religious formulae have ceased to promote the welfare of the generality of mankind, if they no longer minister to the needs of a continually evolving humanity, let them be swept away and relegated to the limbo of obsolescent and forgotten doctrines. Why should these, in a world subject to the immutable law of change and decay, be exempt from the deterioration that must needs overtake every human institution? For legal standards, political and economic theories are solely designed to safeguard the interests of humanity as a whole, and not humanity to be crucified for the preservation of the integrity of any particular law or doctrine.

Banning nuclear weapons, prohibiting the use of poison gases, or outlawing germ warfare will not remove the root causes of war. However important such practical measures obviously are as elements of the peace process, they are in themselves too superficial to exert enduring influence. Peoples are ingenious enough to invent yet other forms of warfare, and to use food, raw materials, finance, industrial power, ideology, and terrorism to subvert one another in an endless quest for supremacy and dominion. Nor can the present massive dislocation in the affairs of humanity be resolved through the settlement of specific conflicts or disagreements among nations. A genuine universal framework must be adopted. (The Universal House of Justice, *The Promise of World Peace*, ¶24–25)

Philanthropy

Charity is pleasing and praiseworthy in the sight of God and is regarded as a prince among goodly deeds. Consider ye and call to mind that which the All-Merciful hath revealed in the Qur'án: "They prefer them before themselves, though poverty be their own lot. And with such as are preserved from their own covetousness shall it be well."* Viewed in this light, the blessed utterance above is, in truth, the day-star of utterances. Blessed is he who preferreth his brother before himself. Verily, such a man is reckoned, by virtue of the Will of God, the All-Knowing, the All-Wise, with the people of Bahá who dwell in the Crimson Ark. (Bahá'u'lláh, *Tablets of Bahá'u'lláh*, p. 71)

I have seen the good effects of your own philanthropy in America, in various universities, peace gatherings, and associations for the promotion of learning, as I traveled from city to city. Wherefore do I pray on your behalf that you shall ever be encompassed by the bounties and blessings of heaven, and shall perform many philanthropic deeds in East and West. Thus may you gleam as a lighted taper in the Kingdom of God, may attain honor and everlasting life, and shine out as a bright star on the horizon of eternity. ('Abdu'l-Bahá, *Selections from the Writings of 'Abdu'l-Bahá*, no. 79.4)

Strive, therefore, to create love in the hearts in order that they may become glowing and radiant. When that love is shining, it will permeate other hearts even as this electric light illumines its surroundings. When the love of God is established, everything else will be realized. This is the true foundation of all economics. Reflect upon it. Endeavor to become the cause of the attraction of souls rather than to enforce minds. Manifest true economics to the people. Show what love is, what kindness is, what true severance is and generosity. This is the important thing for you to do. Act in accordance with the teachings of Bahá'u'lláh. All His Books will be translated. Now is the time for you

---

* Qur'án 59:9.

to live in accordance with His words. Let your deeds be the real translation of their meaning. Economic questions will not attract hearts. The love of God alone will attract them. Economic questions are most interesting; but the power which moves, controls and attracts the hearts of men is the love of God. ('Abdu'l-Bahá, *The Promulgation of Universal Peace,* pp. 334–35)

In the love of God you must become distinguished from all else. You must become distinguished for loving humanity, for unity and accord, for love and justice. In brief, you must become distinguished in all the virtues of the human world—for faithfulness and sincerity, for justice and fidelity, for firmness and steadfastness, for philanthropic deeds and service to the human world, for love toward every human being, for unity and accord with all people, for removing prejudices and promoting international peace. Finally, you must become distinguished for heavenly illumination and for acquiring the bestowals of God. I desire this distinction for you. This must be the point of distinction among you. ('Abdu'l-Bahá, *The Promulgation of Universal Peace,* pp. 265–66)

4

THE NECESSITY OF JUSTICE

Justice, which consisteth in rendering each his due, dependeth upon and is conditioned by two words: reward and punishment. From the standpoint of justice, every soul should receive the reward of his actions, inasmuch as the peace and prosperity of the world depend thereon, even as He saith, exalted be His glory: "The structure of world stability and order hath been reared upon, and will continue to be sustained by, the twin pillars of reward and punishment."
—Bahá'u'lláh, *Tabernacle of Unity*, no. 2.37

The Purpose of Justice

The light of men is Justice. Quench it not with the contrary winds of oppression and tyranny. The purpose of justice is the appearance of unity among men. The ocean of divine wisdom surgeth within this exalted word, while the books of the world cannot contain its inner significance. Were mankind to be adorned with this raiment, they would behold the daystar of the utterance, "On that day God will satisfy everyone out of His abundance,"* shining resplendent above the horizon of the world. Appreciate ye the value of this utterance; it is a noble fruit that the Tree of the Pen of Glory hath yielded. Happy is the man that giveth ear unto it and observeth its precepts. Verily I say, whatever is sent down from the heaven of the Will of God is the means for the establishment of order in the world and the instrument for

---

* Qur'án 4:129.

97

promoting unity and fellowship among its peoples. Thus hath the Tongue of this Wronged One spoken from His Most Great Prison. (Bahá'u'lláh, *Tablets of Bahá'u'lláh*, pp. 66–67)

That which traineth the world is Justice, for it is upheld by two pillars, reward and punishment. These two pillars are the sources of life to the world. (Bahá'u'lláh, *Tablets of Bahá'u'lláh*, p. 27)

We entreat God to deliver the light of equity and the sun of justice from the thick clouds of waywardness, and cause them to shine forth upon men. No light can compare with the light of justice. The establishment of order in the world and the tranquility of the nations depend upon it. (Bahá'u'lláh, *Epistle to the Son of the Wolf*, p. 28)

Say: "O God, my God! Attire mine head with the crown of justice, and my temple with the ornament of equity. Thou, verily, art the Possessor of all gifts and bounties."

Justice and equity are twin Guardians that watch over men. From them are revealed such blessed and perspicuous words as are the cause of the well-being of the world and the protection of the nations. (Bahá'u'lláh, *Epistle to the Son of the Wolf*, pp. 12–13)

Just as forgiveness is one of the attributes of God's mercy, so is justice one of the attributes of His lordship. The canopy of existence rests upon the pole of justice and not of forgiveness, and the life of mankind depends on justice and not on forgiveness. Thus, if a decree of amnesty were to be enacted henceforth in all countries, the whole world would soon be thrown into disarray and the foundations of human life would be shattered. Like-wise, if the powers of Europe had not resisted the notorious Attila, he would not have left a single soul alive. ('Abdu'l-Bahá, *Some Answered Questions*, no. 77.8)

In sum, the proper functioning of the body politic depends upon justice and not forgiveness. So what Christ meant by forgiveness and magnanimity is not that if another nation were to assail you; burn your homes; plunder your possessions; assault your wives, children, and kin; and violate your honour, you must submit to that tyrannical host and permit them to carry out every manner of iniquity and oppression. Rather, the words of Christ refer to private transactions between two individuals, stating that if one person assaults another, the injured party should forgive. But the body politic must safeguard the rights of man. ('Abdu'l-Bahá, *Some Answered Questions*, no. 77.10)

Globalization itself is an intrinsic feature of the evolution of human society. It has brought into existence a socio-economic culture that, at the practical level, constitutes the world in which the aspirations of the human race will be pursued in the century now opening. . . . The unification of human society, forged by the fires of the twentieth century, is a reality that with every passing day opens breath-taking new possibilities. A reality also being forced on serious minds everywhere, is the claim of justice to be the one means capable of harnessing these great potentialities to the advancement of civilization. It no longer requires the gift of prophecy to realize that the fate of humanity in the century now opening will be determined by the relationship established between these two fundamental forces of the historical process, the inseparable principles of unity and justice. (Prepared under the supervision of the Universal House of Justice, *Century of Light*, pp. 134–35)

Justice is the one power that can translate the dawning consciousness of humanity's oneness into a collective will through which the necessary structures of global community life can be confidently erected. An age that sees the people of the world increasingly gaining access to information of every kind and to a diversity of ideas will find justice asserting itself as the ruling principle of successful social organization. With ever greater frequency, proposals aiming at the development of the planet will have to submit to the candid light of the standards it requires.

At the group level, a concern for justice is the indispensable compass in collective decision-making, because it is the only means by which unity of thought and action can be achieved. Far from encouraging the punitive spirit that has often masqueraded under its name in past ages, justice is the practical expression of awareness that, in the achievement of human progress, the interests of the individual and those of society are inextricably linked. To the extent that justice becomes a guiding concern of human interaction, a consultative climate is encouraged that permits options to be examined dispassionately and appropriate courses of action selected. In such a climate the perennial tendencies toward manipulation and partisanship are far less likely to deflect the decision-making process. (Bahá'í International Community, *The Prosperity Of Humankind*)

The Definition of Justice

O son of man! If thine eyes be turned towards mercy, forsake the things that profit thee and cleave unto that which will profit mankind. And if thine eyes be turned towards justice, choose thou for thy neighbor that which thou choosest for thyself. Humility exalteth man to the heaven of glory and power, whilst pride abaseth him to the depths of wretchedness and degradation. (Bahá'u'lláh, *Tablets of Bahá'u'lláh*, p. 64)

The second attribute of perfection is justice and impartiality. This means to have no regard for one's own personal benefits and selfish advantages, and to carry out the laws of God without the slightest concern for anything else. It means to see one's self as only one of the servants of God, the All-Possessing, and except for aspiring to spiritual distinction, never attempting to be singled out from the others. It means to consider the welfare of the community as one's own. It means, in brief, to regard humanity as a single individual, and one's own self as a member of that corporeal form, and to know of a certainty that if pain or injury afflicts any member of that body, it must inevitably result in suffering for all the rest. ('Abdu'l-Bahá, *The Secret of Divine Civilization*, ¶71)

Oh, friends of God, be living examples of justice! So that by the Mercy of God, the world may see in your actions that you manifest the attributes of justice and mercy.

Justice is not limited, it is a universal quality. Its operation must be carried out in all classes, from the highest to the lowest. Justice must be sacred, and the rights of all the people must be considered. Desire for others only that which you desire for yourselves. Then shall we rejoice in the Sun of Justice, which shines from the Horizon of God.

Each man has been placed in a post of honor, which he must not desert. A humble workman who commits an injustice is as much to blame as a renowned tyrant. Thus we all have our choice between justice and injustice.

I hope that each one of you will become just, and direct your thoughts towards the unity of mankind; that you will never harm your neighbors nor speak ill of any one; that you will respect the rights of all men, and be more concerned for the interests of others than for your own. Thus will you become torches of Divine justice, acting in accordance with the Teaching of Bahá'u'lláh, who, during His life, bore innumerable trials and persecutions in order to show forth to the world of mankind the virtues of the World of Divinity, making it possible for you to realize the supremacy of the spirit, and to rejoice in the Justice of God. ('Abdu'l-Bahá, *Paris Talks*, no. 49.14–19)

Know that justice consists in rendering to each his due. For example, when a workman labours from morning till evening, justice requires that he be paid his wage, but bounty consists in rewarding him even when he has done no work and expended no effort. So when you give alms to a poor man who has made no effort and done nothing for your benefit to deserve it, this is bounty. Thus, Christ besought forgiveness for those responsible for His death: This is called bounty. ('Abdu'l-Bahá, *Some Answered Questions*, no. 76.1)

Individual Obligation to Justice

It beseemeth you to fix your gaze under all conditions upon justice and fairness. In The Hidden Words this exalted utterance hath been revealed from Our Most August Pen:

"O Son of Spirit! The best beloved of all things in My sight is Justice; turn not away therefrom if thou desirest Me, and neglect it not that I may confide in thee. By its aid thou shalt see with thine own eyes and not through the eyes of others, and shalt know of thine own knowledge and not through the knowledge of thy neighbor. Ponder this in thy heart; how it behooveth thee to be. Verily justice is My gift to thee and the sign of My loving-kindness. Set it then before thine eyes." (Bahá'u'lláh, *Tablets of Bahá'u'lláh*, pp. 36–37)

The utterance of God is a lamp, whose light is these words: Ye are the fruits of one tree, and the leaves of one branch. Deal ye one with another with the utmost love and harmony, with friendliness and fellowship. He Who is the Daystar of Truth beareth Me witness! So powerful is the light of unity that it can illuminate the whole earth. The One true God, He Who knoweth all things, Himself testifieth to the truth of these words.

Exert yourselves that ye may attain this transcendent and most sublime station, the station that can insure the protection and security of all mankind. This goal excelleth every other goal, and this aspiration is the monarch of all aspirations. So long, however, as the thick clouds of oppression, which obscure the daystar of justice, remain undispelled, it would be difficult for the glory of this station to be unveiled to men's eyes. (Bahá'u'lláh, *Epistle to the Son of the Wolf*, pp. 14–15)

Time and again have We admonished Our beloved ones to avoid, nay to flee from, anything whatsoever from which the odor of mischief can be detected. The world is in great turmoil, and the minds of its people are in a state of utter confusion. We entreat the Almighty that He may graciously illuminate them with the glory of His Justice, and enable them to discover that which will be profitable unto them at all times and under all conditions. He, verily is the All-Possessing, the Most High. (Bahá'u'lláh, *Gleanings from the Writings of Bahá'u'lláh*, no. 44.11)

They who exhort others unto justice, while themselves committing iniquity, stand accused of falsehood by the inmates of the Kingdom and by those who circle round the throne of their Lord, the Almighty, the Beneficent, for that which their tongues have uttered. Commit not, O people, that which dishonoreth your name and the fair name of the Cause of God amongst men. Beware lest ye approach that which your minds abhor. Fear God and follow not in the footsteps of them that are gone astray. Deal not treacherously with the substance of your neighbor. Be ye trustworthy on earth, and withhold not from the poor the things given unto you by God through His grace. He, verily, will bestow upon you the double of what ye possess. He, in truth, is the All-Bounteous, the Most Generous. (Bahá'u'lláh, *The Summons of the Lord of Hosts*, no. 1.149)

Be fair to yourselves and to others, that the evidences of justice may be revealed, through your deeds, among Our faithful servants. Beware lest ye encroach upon the substance of your neighbor. Prove yourselves worthy of his trust and confidence in you, and withhold not from the poor the gifts which the grace of God hath bestowed upon you. He, verily, shall recompense the charitable, and doubly repay them for what they have bestowed. (Bahá'u'lláh, *Gleanings from the Writings of Bahá'u'lláh*, no. 128.9)

I beseech Thee, O my God, by all the transcendent glory of Thy Name, to clothe Thy loved ones in the robe of justice and to illumine their beings with the light of trustworthiness. Thou art the One that hath power to do as He pleaseth and Who holdeth within His grasp the reins of all things visible and invisible. (Bahá'u'lláh, in *Bahá'í Prayers*, p. 173)

You must neither defraud your neighbor not allow him to defraud you. (The Báb, in Nabíl-i-A'zam, *The Dawn-Breakers*, p. 303)

To attain to true glory and honour, man should exercise justice and equity, forbear to act in an oppressive manner, render service to his government, and work for the good of his fellow-citizens. Were he to seek after aught else but this he would indeed be in manifest loss. ('Abdu'l-Bahá, from a Tablet translated from the Persian, in *The Compilation of Compilations,* vol. II, no. 2072)

The Almighty hath not created in man the claws and teeth of ferocious animals, nay rather hath the human form been fashioned and set with the most comely attributes and adorned with the most perfect virtues. The honor of this creation and the worthiness of this garment therefore require man to have love and affinity for his own kind, nay rather, to act towards all living creatures with justice and equity. ('Abdu'l-Bahá, *Selections from the Writings of 'Abdu'l-Bahá,* no. 225.12)

It is clear from what has already been said that man's glory and greatness do not consist in his being avid for blood and sharp of claw, in tearing down cities and spreading havoc, in butchering armed forces and civilians. What would mean a bright future for him would be his reputation for justice, his kindness to the entire population whether high or low, his building up countries and cities, villages and districts, his making life easy, peaceful and happy for his fellow beings, his laying down fundamental principles for progress, his raising the standards and increasing the wealth of the entire population. ('Abdu'l-Bahá, *The Secret of Divine Civilization,* ¶124)

How long shall we drift on the wings of passion and vain desire; how long shall we spend our days like barbarians in the depths of ignorance and abomination? God has given us eyes, that we may look about us at the world, and lay hold of whatsoever will further civilization and the arts of living. He has given us ears, that we may hear and profit by the wisdom of scholars and philosophers and arise to promote and practice it. Senses and faculties have been bestowed upon us, to be devoted to the service of the general good; so that we, distinguished above all other forms of life for perceptiveness and reason, should labor at all times and along all lines, whether the occasion be great or small, ordinary or extraordinary, until all mankind are safely gathered into the impregnable stronghold of knowledge. We should continually be establishing new bases for human happiness and creating and promoting new instrumentalities toward this end. How excellent, how honorable is man if he arises to fulfil his responsibilities; how wretched and contemptible, if he shuts his eyes to the welfare of society and wastes his precious life in pursuing his own selfish interests and personal advantages. Supreme happiness is man's, and he beholds the signs of God in the world and in the human soul, if he urges on the steed of high endeavor in the arena of civilization and justice. "We will surely show them Our signs in the world and within themselves."* ('Abdu'l-Bahá, *The Secret of Divine Civilization,* ¶6)

Why should man, who is endowed with the sense of justice and sensibilities of conscience, be willing that one of the members of the human family should be rated and considered as subordinate? ('Abdu'l-Bahá, *The Promulgation of Universal Peace,* p. 149)

Mere knowledge of principles is not sufficient. We all know and admit that justice is good, but there is need of volition and action to carry out and manifest it. ('Abdu'l-Bahá, *The Promulgation of Universal Peace,* p. 167)

"Equity," He [Bahá'u'lláh] also has written, "is the most fundamental among human virtues. The evaluation of all things must needs depend upon it." And again, "Observe equity in your judgment, ye men of understanding heart! He that is unjust in his judgment is destitute of the characteristics that distinguish man's station." "Beautify your tongues, O people," He further admonishes them, "with truthfulness, and adorn your souls with the

---

* Qur'án 41:53.

ornament of honesty. Beware, O people, that ye deal not treacherously with anyone. Be ye the trustees of God amongst His creatures, and the emblems of His generosity amidst His people." (Shoghi Effendi, *The Advent of Divine Justice*, ¶39)

Justice: A Divine Law

Know verily that the essence of justice and the source thereof are both embodied in the ordinances prescribed by Him Who is the Manifestation of the Self of God amongst men, if ye be of them that recognize this truth. He doth verily incarnate the highest, the infallible standard of justice unto all creation. Were His law to be such as to strike terror into the hearts of all that are in heaven and on earth, that law is naught but manifest justice. The fears and agitation which the revelation of this law provokes in men's hearts should indeed be likened to the cries of the suckling babe weaned from his mother's milk, if ye be of them that perceive. Were men to discover the motivating purpose of God's Revelation, they would assuredly cast away their fears, and, with hearts filled with gratitude, rejoice with exceeding gladness. (Bahá'u'lláh, *Gleanings from the Writings of Bahá'u'lláh*, no. 88.1)

If only the laws and precepts of the prophets of God had been believed, understood and followed, wars would no longer darken the face of the earth.

If man had even the rudiments of justice, such a state of things would be impossible. ('Abdu'l-Bahá, *Paris Talks*, no. 37.5–6)

The essence of the matter is that divine justice will become manifest in human conditions and affairs, and all mankind will find comfort and enjoyment in life. It is not meant that all will be equal, for inequality in degree and capacity is a property of nature. Necessarily there will be rich people and also those who will be in want of their livelihood, but in the aggregate community there will be equalization and readjustment of values and interests. In the future there will be no very rich nor extremely poor. There will be an equilibrium of interests, and a condition will be established which will make both rich and poor comfortable and content. ('Abdu'l-Bahá, *The Promulgation of Universal Peace*, p. 183)

"Know thou, of a truth," He [Bahá'u'lláh] significantly affirms, "these great oppressions that have befallen the world are preparing it for the advent of the Most Great Justice." "Say," He again asserts, "He hath appeared with that Justice wherewith mankind hath been adorned, and yet the people are, for the most part, asleep." . . . "No radiance," He declares, "can compare with that of justice. The organization of the world and the tranquility of mankind depend upon it." . . . "Justice and equity," is yet another assertion, "are two guardians for the protection of man. They have appeared arrayed in their mighty and sacred names to maintain the world in uprightness and protect the nations." "Bestir yourselves, O people," is His emphatic warning, "in anticipation of the days of Divine justice, for the promised hour is now come. Beware lest ye fail to apprehend its import, and be accounted among the erring." "The day is approaching," He similarly has written, "when the faithful will behold the daystar of justice shining in its full splendor from the dayspring of glory." "The shame I was made to bear," He significantly remarks, "hath uncovered the glory with which the whole of creation had been invested, and through the cruelties I have endured, the daystar of justice hath manifested itself, and shed its splendor upon men." "The world," He again has written, "is in great turmoil, and the minds of its people are in a state of utter confusion. We entreat the Almighty that He may graciously illuminate them with the glory of His Justice, and enable them to discover that which will be profitable unto them at all times and under all conditions." And again, "There can be no doubt whatever that if the daystar of justice, which the clouds of tyranny have obscured, were to shed its light upon men, the face of the earth would be completely transformed."

"God be praised!" 'Abdu'l-Bahá, in His turn, exclaims, "The sun of justice hath risen above the horizon of Bahá'u'lláh. For in His Tablets the foundations of such a justice have been laid as no mind hath, from the beginning of creation, conceived." "The canopy of existence," He further explains, "resteth upon the pole of justice, and not of forgiveness, and the life of mankind dependeth on justice and not on forgiveness."

Small wonder, therefore, that the Author of the Bahá'í Revelation should have chosen to associate the name and title of that House [the Universal House of Justice], which is to be the crowning glory of His administrative institutions, not with forgiveness but with justice, to have made justice the only basis and the permanent foundation of His Most Great Peace, and to have proclaimed it in His Hidden Words as "the best beloved of all things" in His sight. It is to the American believers, particularly, that I feel urged to direct this fervent plea to ponder in their hearts the implications of this moral rectitude, and to uphold, with heart and soul and uncompromisingly, both individually and collectively, this sublime standard—a standard of which justice is so essential and potent an element. (Shoghi Effendi, *The Advent of Divine Justice*, ¶42–44)

5

ON WEALTH AND POVERTY

The essence of wealth is love for Me; whoso loveth Me is the possessor of all things, and he that loveth Me not is indeed of the poor and needy.
—Bahá'u'lláh, *Tablets of Bahá'u'lláh*, p. 156

Wealth and the Wealthy

O Ye Rich Ones on Earth! The poor in your midst are My trust; guard ye My trust, and be not intent only on your own ease. (Bahá'u'lláh, The Hidden Words, Persian, no. 54)

O Children of Dust! Tell the rich of the midnight sighing of the poor, lest heedlessness lead them into the path of destruction, and deprive them of the Tree of Wealth. To give and to be generous are attributes of Mine; well is it with him that adorneth himself with My virtues. (Bahá'u'lláh, The Hidden Words, Persian, no. 49)

Deal not treacherously with the substance of your neighbor. Be ye trustworthy on earth, and withhold not from the poor the things given unto you by God through His grace. He, verily will bestow upon you the double of what ye possess. (Bahá'u'lláh, *Epistle to the Son of the Wolf,* p. 54)

They who are possessed of riches, however, must have the utmost regard for the poor, for great is the honor destined by God for those poor who are steadfast in patience. By My life! There is no honor, except what God may

109

please to bestow, that can compare to this honor. Great is the blessedness awaiting the poor that endure patiently and conceal their sufferings, and well is it with the rich who bestow their riches on the needy and prefer them before themselves. (Bahá'u'lláh, *Gleanings from the Writings of Bahá'u'lláh*, no. 100.4)

If ye meet the abased or the downtrodden, turn not away disdainfully from them, for the King of Glory ever watcheth over them and surroundeth them with such tenderness as none can fathom except them that have suffered their wishes and desires to be merged in the Will of your Lord, the Gracious, the All-Wise. O ye rich ones of the earth! Flee not from the face of the poor that lieth in the dust, nay rather befriend him and suffer him to recount the tale of the woes with which God's inscrutable Decree hath caused him to be afflicted. By the righteousness of God! Whilst ye consort with him, the Concourse on high will be looking upon you, will be interceding for you, will be extolling your names and glorifying your action. Blessed are the learned that pride not themselves on their attainments; and well is it with the righteous that mock not the sinful, but rather conceal their misdeeds, so that their own shortcomings may remain veiled to men's eyes. (Bahá'u'lláh, *Gleanings from the Writings of Bahá'u'lláh,* no. 145.1)

O Son of Spirit! Vaunt not thyself over the poor, for I lead him on his way and behold thee in thy evil plight and confound thee for evermore. (Bahá'u'lláh, The Hidden Words, Arabic, no. 25)

O ye rich ones on earth! If ye encounter one who is poor, treat him not disdainfully. Reflect upon that whereof ye were created. Every one of you was created of a sorry germ. (Bahá'u'lláh, *Epistle to the Son of the Wolf,* p. 55)

Blessed is the ruler who succoureth the captive, and the rich one who careth for the poor, and the just one who secureth from the wrong doer the rights of the downtrodden, and happy the trustee who observeth that which the

Ordainer, the Ancient of Days hath prescribed unto him. (Bahá'u'lláh, *Tablets of Bahá'u'lláh*, p. 70)

O ye that are the exponents of generosity and the manifestations thereof! Be generous unto them whom ye find in manifest poverty. O ye that are possessed of riches! Take heed lest outward appearance deter you from benevolent deeds in the path of God, the Lord of all mankind.

. . . Say: Pride not yourselves on earthly riches ye possess. Reflect upon your end and upon the recompense of your works that hath been ordained in the Book of God, the Exalted, the Mighty. Blessed is the rich man whom earthly possessions have been powerless to hinder from turning unto God, the Lord of all names. Verily he is accounted among the most distinguished of men before God, the Gracious, the All-Knowing. (Bahá'u'lláh, in *The Compilation of Compilations*, vol. I, no. 1123)

Every man of discernment, while walking upon the earth, feeleth indeed abashed, inasmuch as he is fully aware that the thing which is the source of his prosperity, his wealth, his might, his exaltation, his advancement and power is, as ordained by God, the very earth which is trodden beneath the feet of all men. There can be no doubt that whoever is cognizant of this truth, is cleansed and sanctified from all pride, arrogance, and vainglory. (Bahá'u'lláh, *Epistle to the Son of the Wolf*, p. 44)

Bahá'u'lláh, likewise, commanded the rich to give freely to the poor. In the Kitáb-i-Aqdas it is further written by Him that those who have a certain amount of income must give one-fifth of it to God, the Creator of heaven and earth. ('Abdu'l-Bahá, *The Promulgation of Universal Peace*, p. 303)

Wealth as a Spiritual Test

O Son of Man! Thou dost wish for gold and I desire thy freedom from it. Thou thinkest thyself rich in its possession, and I recognize thy wealth in thy sanctity therefrom. By My life! This is My knowledge, and that is thy fancy; how can My way accord with thine? (Bahá'u'lláh, The Hidden Words, Arabic, no. 56)

O Son of Being! Busy not thyself with this world, for with fire We test the gold, and with gold We test Our servants. (Bahá'u'lláh, The Hidden Words, Arabic, no. 55)

O Ye that Pride Yourselves on Mortal Riches! Know ye in truth that wealth is a mighty barrier between the seeker and his desire, the lover and his beloved. The rich, but for a few, shall in no wise attain the court of His presence nor enter the city of content and resignation. Well is it then with him, who, being rich, is not hindered by his riches from the eternal kingdom, nor deprived by them of imperishable dominion. By the Most Great Name! The splendor of such a wealthy man shall illuminate the dwellers of heaven even as the sun enlightens the people of the earth! (Bahá'u'lláh, The Hidden Words, Persian, no. 53)

Verily, the thing that deterreth you, in this day, from God is worldliness in its essence. Eschew it, and approach the Most Sublime Vision, this shining and resplendent Seat. Blessed is he who alloweth nothing whatsoever to intervene between him and his Lord. No harm, assuredly, can befall him if he partaketh with justice of the benefits of this world, inasmuch as We have created all things for such of Our servants as truly believe in God. (Bahá'u'lláh, *The Summons of the Lord of Hosts*, no. 1.146)

O Son of Passion! Cleanse thyself from the defilement of riches and in perfect peace advance into the realm of poverty; that from the well-spring of detachment thou mayest quaff the wine of immortal life. (Bahá'u'lláh, The Hidden Words, Persian, no. 55)

It should not be imagined that the writer's earlier remarks constitute a denunciation of wealth or a commendation of poverty. Wealth is praiseworthy in the highest degree, if it is acquired by an individual's own efforts and the grace of God, in commerce, agriculture, art and industry, and if it be expended for philanthropic purposes. Above all, if a judicious and resourceful individual should initiate measures which would universally enrich the masses of the people, there could be no undertaking greater than this, and it would rank in the sight of God as the supreme achievement, for such a benefactor would supply the needs and insure the comfort and well-being of a great multitude. Wealth is most commendable, provided the entire population is wealthy. If, however, a few have inordinate riches while the rest are impoverished, and no fruit or benefit accrues from that wealth, then it is only a liability to its possessor. If, on the other hand, it is expended for the promotion of knowledge, the founding of elementary and other schools, the encouragement of art and industry, the training of orphans and the poor—in brief, if it is dedicated to the welfare of society—its possessor will stand out before God and man as the most excellent of all who live on earth and will be accounted as one of the people of paradise. ('Abdu'l-Bahá, *The Secret of Divine Civilization*, ¶46)

What could be better before God than thinking of the poor? For the poor are beloved by our heavenly Father. When Christ came upon the earth, those who believed in Him and followed Him were the poor and lowly, showing that the poor were near to God. When a rich man believes and follows the Manifestation of God, it is a proof that his wealth is not an obstacle and does not prevent him from attaining the pathway of salvation. After he has been tested and tried, it will be seen whether his possessions are a hindrance in his religious life. But the poor are especially beloved of God. Their lives are full of difficulties, their trials continual, their hopes are in God alone. Therefore, you must assist the poor as much as possible, even by sacrifice of yourself. No deed of man is greater before God than helping the poor. Spiritual conditions are not dependent upon the possession of worldly treasures or the absence of them. When one is physically destitute, spiritual thoughts are more likely. Poverty is a stimulus toward God. Each one of you must have great consideration for the poor and render them assistance. Organize in an effort to help them and prevent increase of poverty. The greatest means for prevention is that whereby the laws of the community will be so framed and enacted that it will not be possible for a few to be millionaires and many destitute. ('Abdu'l-Bahá, *The Promulgation of Universal Peace*, p. 301)

The Insecurity of Wealth

O Son of Man! Should prosperity befall thee, rejoice not, and should abasement come upon thee, grieve not, for both shall pass away and be no more. (Bahá'u'lláh, The Hidden Words, Arabic, no. 52)

O peoples of the earth! . . . Perchance ye may not be consumed by the fire of self and passion, nor allow the vain and worthless objects of this nether world to withhold you from Him Who is the Eternal Truth. Glory and abasement, riches and poverty, tranquility and tribulation, all will pass away, and all the peoples of the earth will erelong be laid to rest in their tombs. It behooveth therefore every man of insight to fix his gaze upon the goal of eternity, that perchance by the grace of Him Who is the Ancient King he may attain unto the immortal Kingdom and abide beneath the shade of the Tree of His Revelation. (Bahá'u'lláh, *The Summons of the Lord of Hosts*, no. 3.20)

Say: Rejoice not in the things ye possess; tonight they are yours, tomorrow others will possess them. Thus warneth you He Who is the All-Knowing, the All-Informed. Say: Can ye claim that what ye own is lasting or secure? Nay! By Myself, the All-Merciful. The days of your life flee away as a breath of wind, and all your pomp and glory shall be folded up as were the pomp and glory of those gone before you. Reflect, O people! What hath become of your bygone days, your lost centuries? Happy the days that have been consecrated to the remembrance of God, and blessed the hours which have been spent in praise of Him Who is the All-Wise. By My life! Neither the pomp of the mighty, nor the wealth of the rich, nor even the ascendancy of the ungodly will endure. All will perish, at a word from Him. He, verily, is the All-Powerful, the All-Compelling, the Almighty. What advantage is there in the earthly things which men possess? That which shall profit them, they have utterly neglected. Erelong, they will awake from their slumber, and find themselves unable to obtain that which hath escaped them in the days of their Lord, the Almighty, the All-Praised. Did they but know it, they would renounce their all, that their names may be mentioned before His throne. They, verily, are accounted among the dead. (Bahá'u'lláh, The Kitáb-i-Aqdas, ¶40)

They that are possessed of wealth and invested with authority and power must show the profoundest regard for religion. In truth, religion is a radiant light and an impregnable stronghold for the protection and welfare of the peoples of the world, for the fear of God impelleth man to hold fast to that which is good, and shun all evil. Should the lamp of religion be obscured, chaos and confusion will ensue, and the lights of fairness and justice, of tranquility and peace cease to shine. Unto this will bear witness every man of true understanding. (Bahá'u'lláh, *Tablets of Bahá'u'lláh*, p. 125)

Every soul seeketh an object and cherisheth a desire, and day and night striveth to attain his aim. One craveth riches, another thirsteth for glory and still another yearneth for fame, for art, for prosperity and the like. Yet finally all are doomed to loss and disappointment. One and all they leave behind them all that is theirs and empty-handed hasten to the realm beyond, and all their labors shall be in vain. To dust they shall all return, denuded, depressed, disheartened and in utter despair.

But, praised be the Lord, thou art engaged in that which secureth for thee a gain that shall eternally endure; and that is naught but thine attraction to the Kingdom of God, thy faith, and thy knowledge, the enlightenment of thine heart, and thine earnest endeavor to promote the Divine Teachings.

Verily this gift is imperishable and this wealth is a treasure from on high! ('Abdu'l-Bahá, *Selections from the Writings of 'Abdu'l-Bahá*, no. 176.1–3)

True Wealth

. . . man should know his own self and recognize that which leadeth unto loftiness or lowliness, glory or abasement, wealth or poverty. Having attained the stage of fulfilment and reached his maturity, man standeth in need of wealth, and such wealth as he acquireth through crafts or professions is commendable and praiseworthy in the estimation of men of wisdom, and especially in the eyes of servants who dedicate themselves to the education of the world and to the edification of its peoples. They are, in truth, cup-bearers of the life-giving water of knowledge and guides unto the ideal way. They direct the peoples of the world to the straight path and acquaint them with that which is conducive to human upliftment and exaltation. The straight path is the one which guideth man to the dayspring of perception and to the dawning-place of true understanding and leadeth him to that which will redound to glory, honor and greatness. (Bahá'u'lláh, *Tablets of Bahá'u'lláh*, pp. 34–35)

Be generous in prosperity, and thankful in adversity. Be worthy of the trust of thy neighbor, and look upon him with a bright and friendly face. Be a treasure to the poor, an admonisher to the rich, an answerer of the cry of the needy, a preserver of the sanctity of thy pledge. Be fair in thy judgment, and guarded in thy speech. Be unjust to no man, and show all meekness to all men. Be as a lamp unto them that walk in darkness, a joy to the sorrowful, a sea for the thirsty, a haven for the distressed, an upholder and defender of the victim of oppression. Let integrity and uprightness distinguish all thine acts. Be a home for the stranger, a balm to the suffering, a tower of strength for the fugitive. Be eyes to the blind, and a guiding light unto the feet of the erring. Be an ornament to the countenance of truth, a crown to the brow of fidelity, a pillar of the temple of righteousness, a breath of life to the body of mankind, an ensign of the hosts of justice, a luminary above the horizon of virtue, a dew to the soil of the human heart, an ark on the ocean of knowledge, a sun in the heaven of bounty, a gem on the diadem of wisdom, a shining light in the firmament of thy generation, a fruit upon the tree of humility. (Bahá'u'lláh, *Epistle to the Son of the Wolf,* p. 93)

. . . it is related that on a certain day, one of the companions of Ṣádiq complained of his poverty before him. Whereupon, Ṣádiq, that immortal beauty, made reply: "Verily thou art rich, and hast drunk the draught of wealth." That poverty-stricken soul was perplexed at the words uttered by that luminous countenance, and said: "Where are my riches, I who stand in need of a single coin?" Ṣádiq thereupon observed: "Dost thou not possess our love?" He replied: "Yea, I possess it, O thou scion of the Prophet of God!" And Sadiq asked him saying: "Exchangest thou this love for one thousand dinars?" He answered: "Nay, never will I exchange it, though the world and all that is therein be given me!" Then Ṣádiq remarked: "How can he who possesses such a treasure be called poor?"

This poverty and these riches, this abasement and glory, this dominion, power, and the like, upon which the eyes and hearts of these vain and foolish souls are set,—all these things fade into utter nothingness in that Court! Even as He hath said: "O men! Ye are but paupers in need of God; but God is the Rich, the Self-Sufficing."* By "riches" therefore is meant independence of all else but God, and by "poverty" the lack of things that are of God. (Bahá'u'lláh, The Kitáb-i-Íqán, ¶142–43)

The beginning of magnanimity is when man expendeth his wealth on himself, on his family and on the poor among his brethren in his Faith.

The essence of wealth is love for Me; whoso loveth Me is the possessor of all things, and he that loveth Me not is indeed of the poor and needy. This is that which the Finger of Glory and Splendor hath revealed. (Bahá'u'lláh, *Tablets of Bahá'u'lláh,* p. 156)

---

* Qur'án 35:15.

ON WEALTH AND POVERTY

Say: I swear by God! No one is despised in the sight of the Almighty for being poor. Rather is he exalted, if he is found to be of them who are patient. (Bahá'u'lláh, *The Compilation of Compilations,* vol. I, no. 1123)

O Son of Being! If poverty overtake thee, be not sad; for in time the Lord of wealth shall visit thee. Fear not abasement, for glory shall one day rest on thee. (Bahá'u'lláh, The Hidden Words, Arabic, no. 53)

Glory be unto Thee, O Lord! Although Thou mayest cause a person to be destitute of all earthly possessions, and from the beginning of his life until his ascension unto Thee he may be reduced to poverty through the operation of Thy decree, yet wert Thou to have brought him forth from the Tree of Thy love, such a bounty would indeed be far better for him than all the things Thou hast created in heaven and earth and whatsoever lieth between them; inasmuch as he will inherit the heavenly home, through the revelation of Thy favors, and will partake of the goodly gifts Thou hast provided therein; for the things which are with Thee are inexhaustible. This indeed is Thy blessing which according to the good-pleasure of Thy Will Thou dost bestow on those who tread the path of Thy love.

How numerous the souls who in former times were put to death for Thy sake, and in whose names all men now pride themselves; and how vast the number of those whom Thou didst enable to acquire earthly fortunes, and who amassed them while they were deprived of Thy Truth, and who in this day have passed into oblivion. Theirs is a grievous chastisement and a dire punishment. (The Báb, *Selections from the Writings of the Báb,* no. 7.20.1–2)

How great the number of people who deck themselves with robes of silk all their lives, while clad in the garb of fire, inasmuch as they have divested themselves of the raiment of divine guidance and righteousness; and how numerous are those who wear clothes made of cotton or coarse wool throughout their lives, and yet by reason of their being endowed with the vesture of divine guidance and righteousness, are truly attired with the raiment of

118

Paradise and take delight in the good-pleasure of God. Indeed it would be better in the sight of God were ye to combine the two, adorning yourselves with the raiment of divine guidance and righteousness and wearing exquisite silk, if ye can afford to do so. If not, at least act ye not unrighteously, but rather observe piety and virtue. (The Báb, *Selections from the Writings of the Báb*, no. 5.21.1)

Soon will your swiftly-passing days be over, and the fame and riches, the comforts, the joys provided by this rubbish-heap, the world, will be gone without a trace. Summon ye, then, the people to God, and invite humanity to follow the example of the Company on high. Be ye loving fathers to the orphan, and a refuge to the helpless, and a treasury for the poor, and a cure for the ailing. Be ye the helpers of every victim of oppression, the patrons of the disadvantaged. Think ye at all times of rendering some service to every member of the human race. Pay ye no heed to aversion and rejection, to disdain, hostility, injustice: act ye in the opposite way. Be ye sincerely kind, not in appearance only. Let each one of God's loved ones center his attention on this: to be the Lord's mercy to man; to be the Lord's grace. Let him do some good to every person whose path he crosseth, and be of some benefit to him. Let him improve the character of each and all, and reorient the minds of men. In this way, the light of divine guidance will shine forth, and the blessings of God will cradle all mankind: for love is light, no matter in what abode it dwelleth; and hate is darkness, no matter where it may make its nest. O friends of God! That the hidden Mystery may stand revealed, and the secret essence of all things may be disclosed, strive ye to banish that darkness for ever and ever. ('Abdu'l-Bahá, *Selections from the Writings of 'Abdu'l-Bahá*, no. 1.7)

The purpose of the foregoing statements is to demonstrate at least this, that the happiness and greatness, the rank and station, the pleasure and peace, of an individual have never consisted in his personal wealth, but rather in his excellent character, his high resolve, the breadth of his learning, and his ability to solve difficult problems. How well has it been said: "On my back is a garment which, were it sold for a penny, that penny would be worth far more; yet within the garment is a soul which, if you weighed it against all the souls in the world, would prove greater and nobler." ('Abdu'l-Bahá, *The Secret of Divine Civilization,* ¶44)

Bahá'u'lláh hath been made manifest to all mankind and He hath invited all to the table of God, the banquet of Divine bounty. Today, however, most of those who sit at that table are the poor, and this is why Christ hath said blessed are the poor, for riches do prevent the rich from entering the Kingdom; and again, He saith, "It is easier for a camel to go through the eye of a needle, than for a rich man to enter into the Kingdom of God."* If, however, the wealth of this world, and worldly glory and repute, do not block his entry therein, that rich man will be favored at the Holy Threshold and accepted by the Lord of the Kingdom.

In brief, Bahá'u'lláh hath become manifest to educate all the peoples of the world. He is the Universal Educator, whether of the rich or the poor, whether of black or white, or of peoples from east or west, or north or south. ('Abdu'l-Bahá, *Selections from the Writings of 'Abdu'l-Bahá,* no. 163.9–10)

The honour and exaltation of every existing thing are contingent upon certain causes and conditions.

The excellence, adornment, and perfection of the earth consist in this, that through the outpourings of the vernal showers it should become green and verdant; that plants should spring forth; that flowers and herbs should grow; that blossom-filled trees should produce an abundant yield and bring forth fresh and succulent fruit; that gardens should be arrayed; that plains and mountains should don an emerald robe; and that fields and bowers, villages and cities should be decked forth. This is the felicity of the mineral world.

---

* Matthew 19:24; Mark 10:25.

The height of exaltation and perfection of the vegetable world consists in this, that a tree should stand tall beside a stream of fresh water, that a gentle breeze should blow and the sun bestow its warmth upon it, that a gardener should tend it, and that day by day it should grow and yield fruit. But its real felicity consists in progressing into the animal and human worlds and in replacing that which has been consumed in the bodies of animals and men.

The exaltation of the animal world is to possess perfect members, organs, and powers, and to have all its needs supplied. This is the height of its glory, honour, and exaltation. So the supreme felicity of an animal resides in a green and verdant meadow, in a flowing stream of the sweetest water, and in a forest brimming with life. If these things are provided, no greater felicity can be imagined for the animal. For example, were a bird to build its nest in a green and verdant forest, in a pleasant height, upon a mighty tree, and atop a lofty branch, and were it to have at its disposal all the seed and water that it requires, then this would constitute its perfect felicity.

But true felicity for the animal consists in passing from the animal world into the human realm, like the microscopic beings that, through the air and the water, enter into the body of man, are assimilated, and replace that which has been consumed in his body. This is the greatest honour and felicity for the animal world, and no greater honour can be conceived for it.

Therefore, it is clear and evident that such material ease, comfort, and abundance are the height of felicity for minerals, plants, and animals. And indeed no wealth, prosperity, comfort, or ease in our material world can equal the wealth of a bird, for it has all the expanse of the fields and mountains for a dwelling place; all the seed and harvests for wealth and sustenance; and all the lands, villages, meadows, pastures, forests, and wilderness for possessions. Now which is the richer—this bird or the wealthiest of men? For no matter how many seeds that bird may gather up or give away, its wealth does not diminish.

Then it is clear that the honour and exaltation of man cannot reside solely in material delights and earthly benefits. This material felicity is wholly secondary, while the exaltation of man resides primarily in such virtues and attainments as are the adornments of the human reality. These consist in divine blessings, heavenly bounties, heartfelt emotions, the love and knowledge of God, the education of the people, the perceptions of the mind, and the discoveries of science. They consist in justice and equity, truthfulness and benevolence, inner courage and innate humanity, safeguarding the rights of others and preserving the sanctity of covenants and agreements. They consist in rectitude of conduct under all circumstances, love of truth under all conditions, self-abnegation for the good of all people, kindness and compassion for all nations, obedience to the teachings of God, service to the heavenly Kingdom, guidance for all mankind, and education for all races and nations. This is the felicity of the human world! This is the exaltation of man in the contingent realm! This is eternal life and heavenly honour!

These gifts, however, do not manifest themselves in the reality of man save through a celestial and divine power and through the heavenly teachings, for they require a supernatural power. Traces of these perfections may well appear in the world of nature, but they are as fleeting and ephemeral as rays of sunlight upon the wall.

As the compassionate Lord has crowned the head of man with such a refulgent diadem, we must strive that its luminous gems may cast their light upon the whole world. ('Abdu'l-Bahá, *Some Answered Questions*, no. 15.1–9)

Consider the birds in the forest and jungle: how they build their nests high in the swaying treetops, build them with the utmost skill and beauty—swinging, rocking in the morning breezes, drinking the pure, sweet water, enjoying the most enchanting views as they fly here and there high overhead, singing joyously—all without labor, free from worry, care and forebodings. If man's life be confined to the elemental, physical world of enjoyment, one lark is nobler, more admirable than all humanity because its livelihood is prepared, its condition complete, its accomplishment perfect and natural.

But the life of man is not so restricted; it is divine, eternal, not mortal and sensual. For him a spiritual existence and livelihood is prepared and ordained in the divine creative plan. His life is intended to be a life of spiritual enjoyment to which the animal can never attain. This enjoyment depends upon the acquisition of heavenly virtues. The sublimity of man is his attainment of the knowledge of God. The bliss of man is the acquiring of heavenly bestowals, which descend upon him in the outflow of the bounty of God. The happiness of man is in the fragrance of the love of God. This is the highest pinnacle of attainment in the human world. How preferable to the animal and its hopeless kingdom!

Therefore, consider how base a nature it reveals in man that, notwithstanding the favors showered upon him by God, he should lower himself into the animal sphere, be wholly occupied with material needs, attached to this mortal realm, imagining that the greatest happiness is to attain wealth in this world. How purposeless! How debased is such a nature! God has created man in order that he may be a dove of the Kingdom, a heavenly candle, a recipient of eternal life. God has created man in order that he may be resuscitated through the breaths of the Holy Spirit and become the light of the world. How debased the soul which can find enjoyment in this darkness, occupied with itself, the captive of self and passion, wallowing in the mire of the material world! How degraded is such a nature! What an ignorance this is! What a blindness! How glorious the station of man who has partaken of the heavenly food and built the temple of his everlasting residence in the world of heaven!

The Manifestations of God have come into the world to free man from these bonds and chains of the world of nature. Although They walked upon the earth, They lived in heaven. They were not concerned about material sustenance and prosperity of this world. Their bodies were subjected to inconceivable distress, but Their spirits ever soared in the highest realms of ecstasy. The purpose of Their coming, Their teaching and suffering was the freedom of man from himself. Shall we, therefore, follow in Their footsteps, escape from this cage of the body or continue subject to its tyranny? Shall we pursue the phantom of a mortal happiness which does not exist or turn toward the tree of life and the joys of its eternal fruits? ('Abdu'l-Bahá, *The Promulgation of Universal Peace*, pp. 257–58)

Man is he who forgets his own interests for the sake of others. His own comfort he forfeits for the well-being of all. Nay, rather, his own life must he be willing to forfeit for the life of mankind. Such a man is the honor of the world of humanity. Such a man is the glory of the world of mankind. Such a man is the one who wins eternal bliss. Such a man is near to the threshold of God. Such a man is the very manifestation of eternal happiness. Otherwise, men are like animals, exhibiting the same proclivities and propensities as the world of animals. What distinction is there? What prerogatives, what perfection? None whatever! Animals are better even thinking only of themselves and negligent of the needs of others.

Consider how the greatest men in the world—whether among prophets or philosophers—all have forfeited their own comfort, have sacrificed their own pleasure for the well-being of humanity. They have sacrificed their own lives for the body politic. They have sacrificed their own wealth for that of the general welfare. They have forfeited their own honor for the honor of mankind. Therefore, it becomes evident that this is the highest attainment for the world of humanity. ('Abdu'l-Bahá, *The Promulgation of Universal Peace,* pp. 441–42)

The Poverty of the Prophets of God

And now regarding His words, that the Son of man shall "come in the clouds of heaven." By the term "clouds" is meant those things that are contrary to the ways and desires of men. Even as He hath revealed in the verse already quoted: "As oft as an Apostle cometh unto you with that which your souls desire not, ye swell with pride, accusing some of being impostors and slaying others."* These "clouds" signify, in one sense, the annulment of laws, the abrogation of former Dispensations, the repeal of rituals and customs current amongst men, the exalting of the illiterate faithful above the learned opposers of the Faith. In another sense, they mean the appearance of that

* Qur'án 2:87.

immortal Beauty in the image of mortal man, with such human limitations as eating and drinking, poverty and riches, glory and abasement, sleeping and waking, and such other things as cast doubt in the minds of men, and cause them to turn away. All such veils are symbolically referred to as "clouds."

These are the "clouds" that cause the heavens of the knowledge and understanding of all that dwell on earth to be cloven asunder. Even as He hath revealed: "On that day shall the heaven be cloven by the clouds."* Even as the clouds prevent the eyes of men from beholding the sun, so do these things hinder the souls of men from recognizing the light of the divine Luminary. To this beareth witness that which hath proceeded out of the mouth of the unbelievers as revealed in the sacred Book: "And they have said: 'What manner of apostle is this? He eateth food, and walketh the streets. Unless an angel be sent down and take part in His warnings, we will not believe.'"** Other Prophets, similarly, have been subject to poverty and afflictions, to hunger, and to the ills and chances of this world. As these holy Persons were subject to such needs and wants, the people were, consequently, lost in the wilds of misgivings and doubts, and were afflicted with bewilderment and perplexity. How, they wondered, could such a person be sent down from God, assert His ascendancy over all the peoples and kindreds of the earth, and claim Himself to be the goal of all creation,—even as He hath said: "But for Thee, I would not have created all that are in heaven and on earth,"—and yet be subject to such trivial things? You must undoubtedly have been informed of the tribulations, the poverty, the ills, and the degradation that have befallen every Prophet of God and His companions. You must have heard how the heads of their followers were sent as presents unto different cities, how grievously they were hindered from that whereunto they were commanded. Each and every one of them fell a prey to the hands of the enemies of His Cause, and had to suffer whatsoever they decreed. (Bahá'u'lláh, The Kitáb-i-Íqán, ¶79–80)

---

* Qur'án 25:25.
** Qur'án 25:7.

The highest station, the supreme sphere, the noblest, most sublime position in creation, whether visible or invisible, whether alpha or omega, is that of the Prophets of God, notwithstanding the fact that for the most part they have to outward seeming been possessed of nothing but their own poverty. In the same way, ineffable glory is set apart for the Holy Ones and those who are nearest to the Threshold of God, although such as these have never for a moment concerned themselves with material gain. Then comes the station of those just kings whose fame as protectors of the people and dispensers of Divine justice has filled the world, whose name as powerful champions of the people's rights has echoed through creation. These give no thought to amassing enormous fortunes for themselves; they believe, rather, that their own wealth lies in enriching their subjects. To them, if every individual citizen has affluence and ease, the royal coffers are full. They take no pride in gold and silver, but rather in their enlightenment and their determination to achieve the universal good. ('Abdu'l-Bahá, *The Secret of Divine Civilization,* ¶38)

You must be thankful to God that you are poor, for Jesus Christ has said, "Blessed are the poor." He never said, "Blessed are the rich." He said, too, that the Kingdom is for the poor and that it is easier for a camel to enter a needle's eye than for a rich man to enter God's Kingdom. Therefore, you must be thankful to God that although in this world you are indigent, yet the treasures of God are within your reach; and although in the material realm you are poor, yet in the Kingdom of God you are precious. Jesus Himself was poor. He did not belong to the rich. He passed His time in the desert, traveling among the poor, and lived upon the herbs of the field. He had no place to lay His head, no home. He was exposed in the open to heat, cold and frost—to inclement weather of all kinds—yet He chose this rather than riches. If riches were considered a glory, the Prophet Moses would have chosen them; Jesus would have been a rich man. When Jesus Christ appeared, it was the poor who first accepted Him, not the rich. Therefore, you are the disciples of Jesus Christ; you are His comrades, for He outwardly was poor, not rich. Even this earth's happiness does not depend upon wealth. You will find many of the wealthy exposed to dangers and troubled by difficulties, and in their last moments upon the bed of death there remains the regret that they must be separated from that to which their hearts are so attached. They come into this world naked, and they must go from it naked. All they possess they must leave behind and pass away solitary, alone. Often at the time of death their souls are filled with remorse; and worst of all, their hope in the mercy of God is less than ours. Praise be to God! Our hope is in the mercy of God, and there is no doubt that the divine compassion is bestowed upon the poor. Jesus Christ said so; Bahá'u'lláh said so. While Bahá'u'lláh was in Baghdád, still in possession of great wealth, He left all He had and went alone from the city, living two years among the poor. They were His comrades. He ate with them, slept with them and gloried in being one of them. He chose for one of His names the title of The Poor One and often in His Writings refers to Himself as Darvish, which in Persian means poor; and of this title He was very proud. He admonished all that we must be the servants of the poor, helpers of the poor, remember the sorrows of the poor, associate with them; for thereby we may inherit the Kingdom of heaven. God has not said that there are mansions prepared for us if we pass our time associating with the rich, but He has said there are many mansions prepared for the servants of the poor, for the poor are very dear to God. The mercies and bounties of God are with them. The rich are mostly negligent, inattentive, steeped in worldliness, depending upon their means, whereas the poor are dependent upon God, and their reliance is upon Him, not upon themselves. Therefore, the poor are nearer the threshold of God and His throne.

Jesus was a poor man. One night when He was out in the fields, the rain began to fall. He had no place to go for shelter so He lifted His eyes toward heaven, saying, "O Father! For the birds of the air Thou hast created nests, for the sheep a fold, for the animals dens, for the fish places of refuge, but for Me Thou hast provided no shelter. There is no place where I may lay My head. My bed consists of the cold ground; My lamps at night are the stars, and My food is the grass of the field. Yet who upon earth is richer than I?

For the greatest blessing Thou hast not given to the rich and mighty but unto Me, for Thou hast given Me the poor. To me Thou hast granted this blessing. They are Mine. Therefore am I the richest man on earth."

So, my comrades, you are following in the footsteps of Jesus Christ. Your lives are similar to His life; your attitude is like unto His; you resemble Him more than the rich do. Therefore, we will thank God that we have been so blessed with real riches. . . . ('Abdu'l-Bahá, *The Promulgation of Universal Peace*, pp. 44–46)

The Blessed Perfection, Bahá'u'lláh, belonged to the nobility of Persia. From earliest childhood He was distinguished among His relatives and friends. . . .

Until His father passed away, Bahá'u'lláh did not seek position or political station notwithstanding His connection with the government. This occasioned surprise and comment. It was frequently said, "How is it that a young man of such keen intelligence and subtle perception does not seek lucrative appointments? As a matter of fact, every position is open to him." This is an historical statement fully attested by the people of Persia.

He was most generous, giving abundantly to the poor. None who came to Him were turned away. The doors of His house were open to all. He always had many guests. This unbounded generosity was conducive to greater astonishment from the fact that He sought neither position nor prominence. In commenting upon this His friends said He would become impoverished, for His expenses were many and His wealth becoming more and more limited. "Why is he not thinking of his own affairs?" they inquired of each other; but some who were wise declared, "This personage is connected with another world; he has something sublime within him that is not evident now; the day is coming when it will be manifested." In truth, the Blessed Perfection was a refuge for every weak one, a shelter for every fearing one, kind to every indigent one, lenient and loving to all creatures.

He became well-known in regard to these qualities before the Báb appeared. Then Bahá'u'lláh declared the Báb's mission to be true and promulgated His teachings. The Báb announced that the greater Manifestation would take place after Him and called the Promised One "Him Whom God shall make manifest," saying that nine years later the reality of His own mission would become apparent. In His writings He stated that in the ninth year this expected One would be known; in the ninth year they would attain to all glory and felicity; in the ninth year they would advance rapidly. . . . The Báb was martyred in Tabríz; and Bahá'u'lláh, exiled into 'Iráq in 1852, announced Himself in Baghdád. For the Persian government had decided that as long as He remained in Persia the peace of the country would be disturbed; therefore, He was exiled in the expectation that Persia would become quiet. His banishment, however, produced the opposite effect. New tumult arose, and the mention of His greatness and influence spread everywhere throughout the country. The proclamation of His manifestation and mission was made in Baghdád. He called His friends together there and spoke to them of God.

At one point He left the city and went alone into the mountains of Kurdistán, where He made His abode in caves and grottoes. A part of this time He lived in the city of Sulaymáníyyih. Two years passed during which neither His friends nor family knew just where He was.

. . . During this period Bahá'u'lláh lived in poverty. His garments were those of the poor and needy. His food was that of the indigent and lowly. An atmosphere of majesty haloed Him as the sun at midday. Everywhere He was greatly revered and beloved.

After two years He returned to Baghdád. . . .

The Persian government believed the banishment of the Blessed Perfection from Persia would be the extermination of His Cause in that country. These rulers now realized that it spread more rapidly. His prestige increased; His teachings became more widely circulated. The chiefs of Persia then used their influence to have Bahá'u'lláh exiled from Baghdád. He was summoned to Constantinople by the Turkish authorities. While in Constantinople He ignored every restriction, especially the hostility of ministers of state and clergy. The official representatives of Persia again brought their influence to bear upon the Turkish authorities and succeeded in having Bahá'u'lláh banished from Constantinople to Adrianople, the object being to keep Him as far away as possible from Persia and render His communication with that country more difficult. Nevertheless, the Cause still spread and strengthened.

Finally, they consulted together and said, "We have banished Bahá'u'lláh from place to place, but each time he is exiled his cause is more widely extended, his proclamation increases in power, and day by day his lamp is becoming brighter. This is due to the fact that we have exiled him to large cities and populous centers. Therefore, we will send him to a penal colony as a prisoner so that all may know he is the associate of murderers, robbers and criminals; in a short time he and his followers will perish." The Sultan of Turkey then banished Him to the prison of 'Akká in Syria.

When Bahá'u'lláh arrived at 'Akká, through the power of God He was able to hoist His banner. His light at first had been a star; now it became a mighty sun, and the illumination of His Cause expanded from the East to the West. . . .

His Cause spread more and more. The Blessed Perfection was a prisoner twenty-five years. During all this time He was subjected to the indignities and revilement of the people. He was persecuted, mocked and put in chains. In Persia His properties were pillaged and His possessions confiscated. First, there was banishment from Persia to Baghdád, then to Constantinople, then to Adrianople, finally from Rumelia to the prison fortress of 'Akká.

During His lifetime He was intensely active. His energy was unlimited. Scarcely one night was passed in restful sleep. He bore these ordeals, suffered these calamities and difficulties in order that a manifestation of selflessness and service might become apparent in the world of humanity; that the Most Great Peace should become a reality; that human souls might appear as the angels of heaven; that heavenly miracles would be wrought among men; that human faith should be strengthened and perfected; that the precious, priceless bestowal of God—the human mind—might be developed to its fullest capacity in the temple of the body; and that man might become the reflection and likeness of God, even as it hath been revealed in the Bible, "Let us make man in our image."

Briefly, the Blessed Perfection bore all these ordeals and calamities in order that our hearts might become enkindled and radiant, our spirits be glorified, our faults become virtues, our ignorance be transformed into knowledge; in order that we might attain the real fruits of humanity and acquire heavenly graces; in order that, although pilgrims upon earth, we should travel the road of the heavenly Kingdom, and, although needy and poor, we might receive the treasures of eternal life. For this has He borne these difficulties and sorrows.

Trust all to God. The lights of God are resplendent. The blessed Epistles are spreading. The blessed teachings are promulgated throughout the East and West. Soon you will see that the heavenly Words have established the oneness of the world of humanity. The banner of the Most Great Peace has been unfurled, and the great community is appearing. ('Abdu'l-Bahá, *The Promulgation of Universal Peace,* pp. 34–39)

Suffering, of one kind or another, seems to be the portion of man in this world. Even the Beloved ones, the Prophets of God, have never been exempt from the ills that are to be found in our world; poverty, disease, bereavement,—they seem to be part of the polish God employs to make us finer, and enable us to reflect more of His attributes! No doubt in the future, when the foundation of society is laid according to the Divine plan, and men become truly spiritualized, a vast amount of our present ills and problems will be remedied. We who toil now are paving the way for a far better world, and this knowledge must uphold and strengthen us through every trial. (From a letter written on behalf of Shoghi Effendi, dated 3 March 1943, to an individual believer, in *Lights of Guidance,* no. 2049)

A New Economic Order

All the peoples of the world will enjoy like interests, and the poor shall possess a portion of the comforts of life. Just as the rich are surrounded by their luxuries in palaces, the poor will have at least their comfortable and pleasant places of abode; and just as the wealthy enjoy a variety of food, the needy shall have their necessities and no longer live in poverty. In short, a readjustment of the economic order will come about, . . . ('Abdu'l-Bahá, *The Promulgation of Universal Peace,* p. 140)

Now is the beginning of the manifestation of the spiritual power, and inevitably the potency of its life forces will assume greater and greater proportions. Therefore, this twentieth century is the dawn, or beginning, of spiritual illumination, and it is evident that day by day it will advance. It will reach such a degree that spiritual effulgences will overcome the physical, so that divine susceptibilities will overpower material intelligence and the heavenly light dispel and banish earthly darkness. Divine healing shall purify all ills, and the cloud of mercy will pour down its rain. The Sun of Reality will shine, and all the earth shall put on its beautiful green carpet. Among the results of the manifestation of spiritual forces will be that the human world will adapt itself to a new social form, the justice of God will become manifest throughout human affairs, and human equality will be universally established. The poor will receive a great bestowal, and the rich attain eternal happiness. For although at the present time the rich enjoy the greatest luxury and comfort, they are nevertheless deprived of eternal happiness; for eternal happiness is contingent upon giving, and the poor are everywhere in the state of abject need. Through the manifestation of God's great equity the poor of the world will be rewarded and assisted fully, and there will be a readjustment in the economic conditions of mankind so that in the future there will not be the abnormally rich nor the abject poor. The rich will enjoy the privilege of this new economic condition as well as the poor, for owing to certain provisions and restrictions they will not be able to accumulate so much as to be burdened by its management, while the poor will be relieved from the stress of want and misery. ('Abdu'l-Bahá, *The Promulgation of Universal Peace,* pp. 182–83)

6

THE OBLIGATION TO WORK

Man must work with his fellows. Everyone should have some trade, or art or profession, be he rich or poor, and with this he must serve humanity. This service is acceptable as the highest form of worship.
—'Abdu'l-Bahá, *'Abdu'l-Bahá in London,* p. 93

Work in a Spirit of Service is Worship

It is enjoined upon every one of you to engage in some form of occupation, such as crafts, trades and the like. We have graciously exalted your engagement in such work to the rank of worship unto God, the True One. Ponder ye in your hearts the grace and the blessings of God and render thanks unto Him at eventide and at dawn. Waste not your time in idleness and sloth. Occupy yourselves with that which profiteth yourselves and others. Thus hath it been decreed in this Tablet from whose horizon the daystar of wisdom and utterance shineth resplendent. (Bahá'u'lláh, *Tablets of Bahá'u'lláh,* p. 26)

. . . it is incumbent upon everyone, even should he be resident in a particular land for no more than a single day, to become engaged in some craft or trade, or agriculture, and that the very pursuit of such a calling is, in the eyes of the one true God, identical with worship. (Bahá'u'lláh, in "Economics, Agriculture, and Related Subjects," published in *Compilation of Compilations,* vol. III, pp. 5–17)

The man who makes a piece of notepaper to the best of his ability, conscientiously, concentrating all his forces on perfecting it, is giving praise to God. Briefly, all effort and exertion put forth by man from the fullness of his heart is worship, if it is prompted by the highest motives and the will to do service to humanity. This is worship: to serve mankind and to minister to the needs of the people. Service is prayer. A physician ministering to the sick, gently, tenderly, free from prejudice and believing in the solidarity of the human race, he is giving praise. ('Abdu'l-Bahá, *Paris Talks,* no. 55.1)

Unemployment raises similar issues. In most of contemporary thinking, the concept of work has been largely reduced to that of gainful employment aimed at acquiring the means for the consumption of available goods. The system is circular: acquisition and consumption resulting in the maintenance and expansion of the production of goods and, in consequence, in supporting paid employment. Taken individually, all of these activities are essential to the well-being of society. The inadequacy of the overall conception, however, can be read in both the apathy that social commentators discern among large numbers of the employed in every land and the demoralization of the growing armies of the unemployed.

Not surprisingly, therefore, there is increasing recognition that the world is in urgent need of a new "work ethic." Here again, nothing less than insights generated by the creative interaction of the scientific and religious systems of knowledge can produce so fundamental a reorientation of habits and attitudes. Unlike animals, which depend for their sustenance on whatever the environment readily affords, human beings are impelled to express the immense capacities latent within them through productive work designed to meet their own needs and those of others. In acting thus they become participants, at however modest a level, in the processes of the advancement of civilization. They fulfill purposes that unite them with others. To the extent that work is consciously undertaken in a spirit of service to humanity, Bahá'u'lláh says, it is a form of prayer, a means of worshipping God. Every individual has the capacity to see himself or herself in this light, and it is to this inalienable capacity of the self that development strategy must appeal, whatever the nature of the plans being pursued, whatever the rewards they promise. No narrower a perspective will ever call up from the people of the world the magnitude of effort and commitment that the economic tasks ahead will require. (Bahá'í International Community, *The Prosperity of Humankind*)

Work as a Duty
O My Servants! Ye are the trees of My garden; ye must give forth goodly and wondrous fruits, that ye yourselves and others may profit therefrom. Thus it is incumbent on every one to engage in crafts and professions, for therein lies the secret of wealth, O men of understanding! For results depend upon means, and the grace of God shall be all-sufficient unto you. Trees that yield no fruit have been and will ever be for the fire. (Bahá'u'lláh, The Hidden Words, Persian, no. 80)

We have enjoined upon all to become engaged in some trade or profession, and have accounted such occupation to be an act of worship. Before all else, however, thou shouldst receive, as a sign of God's acceptance, the mantle of trustworthiness from the hands of divine favour; for trustworthiness is the chief means of attracting confirmation and prosperity. We entreat God to make of it a radiant and mercifully showering rain-cloud that shall bring success and blessings to thy affairs. He of a truth is the All-Bountiful, the Gracious. (Bahá'u'lláh, in *The Compilation of Compilations*, vol. II, no. 2045)

The best of men are they that earn a livelihood by their calling and spend upon themselves and upon their kindred for the love of God. (Bahá'u'lláh The Hidden Words, Persian, no. 82)

To engage in some profession is highly commendable, for when occupied with work one is less likely to dwell on the unpleasant aspects of life. (Bahá'u'lláh, *Tablets of Bahá'u'lláh*, p. 175)

Please God, the poor may exert themselves and strive to earn the means of livelihood. This is a duty which, in this most great Revelation, hath been prescribed unto every one, and is accounted in the sight of God as a goodly deed. Whoso observeth this duty, the help of the invisible One shall most certainly aid him. He can enrich, through His grace, whomsoever He pleaseth. He, verily, hath power over all things. (Bahá'u'lláh, *Gleanings from the Writings of Bahá'u'lláh*, no. 100.5)

It is well to know that riches are good, but that knowledge will not make a man rich; he must work, he must put his knowledge into practice. ('Abdu'l-Bahá, *'Abdu'l-Bahá in London*, p. 60)

Whatever the progress of the machinery may be, man will have always to toil in order to earn his living. Effort is an inseparable part of man's life. It may take different forms with the changing conditions of the world, but it will be always present as a necessary element in our earthly existence. Life is after all a struggle. Progress is attained through struggle, and without such a struggle life ceases to have a meaning; it becomes even extinct. The progress of machinery has not made effort unnecessary. It has given it a new form, a new outlet. (From a letter written on behalf of Shoghi Effendi, dated 26 December 1935, to an individual believer, in *Lights of Guidance*, no. 1870)

It is obligatory for men and women to engage in a trade or profession. Bahá'u'lláh exalts "engagement in such work" to the "rank of worship" of God. The spiritual and practical significance of this law, and the mutual responsibility of the individual and society for its implementation are explained in a letter written on behalf of Shoghi Effendi:

With reference to Bahá'u'lláh's command concerning the engagement of the believers in some sort of profession: the Teachings are most emphatic on this matter, particularly the statement in the Aqdas to this effect which makes it quite clear that idle people who lack the desire to work can have no place in the new World Order. As a corollary of this principle, Bahá'u'lláh further

136

states that mendicity should not only be discouraged but entirely wiped out from the face of society. It is the duty of those who are in charge of the organization of society to give every individual the opportunity of acquiring the necessary talent in some kind of profession, and also the means of utilizing such a talent, both for its own sake and for the sake of earning the means of his livelihood. Every individual, no matter how handicapped and limited he may be, is under the obligation of engaging in some work or profession, for work, especially when performed in the spirit of service, is according to Bahá'u'lláh a form of worship. It has not only a utilitarian purpose, but has a value in itself, because it draws us nearer to God, and enables us to better grasp His purpose for us in this world. It is obvious, therefore, that the inheritance of wealth cannot make anyone immune from daily work. (The Universal House of Justice, in The Kitáb-i-Aqdas, p. 192)

Work is both a means of livelihood for the individual and a way of contributing to the prosperity of the community as a whole. As such, it helps give meaning to one's life. Therefore, community design must ensure that the creative energies of the individual have a channel of useful employment in which they can be expressed. For his or her part, the individual must assume responsibility in carrying out this trust. Progress in this area will lend great momentum to the elimination of extremes of wealth and poverty in the world. (Bahá'í International Community, "Sustainable Communities in an Integrating World")

Idleness and Begging

O My Servant! The basest of men are they that yield no fruit on earth. Such men are verily counted as among the dead, nay better are the dead in the sight of God than those idle and worthless souls. (Bahá'u'lláh, The Hidden Words, Persian, no. 81)

The most despised of men in the sight of God are those who sit idly and beg. Hold ye fast unto the cord of material means, placing your whole trust in

God, the Provider of all means. When anyone occupieth himself in a craft or trade, such occupation itself is regarded in the estimation of God as an act of worship; and this is naught but a token of His infinite and all-pervasive bounty. (Bahá'u'lláh, *Tablets of Bahá'u'lláh*, p. 26)

It is unlawful to beg, and it is forbidden to give to him who beggeth. All have been enjoined to earn a living, and as for those who are incapable of doing so, it is incumbent on the Deputies of God and on the wealthy to make adequate provision for them. Keep ye the statutes and commandments of God; nay, guard them as ye would your very eyes, and be not of those who suffer grievous loss. (Bahá'u'lláh, The Kitáb-i-Aqdas, ¶147)

In a Tablet 'Abdu'l-Bahá expounds the meaning of this verse. He states that "mendicancy is forbidden and that giving charity to people who take up begging as their profession is also prohibited." He further points out in that same Tablet: "The object is to uproot mendicancy altogether. However, if a person is incapable of earning a living, is stricken by dire poverty or becometh helpless, then it is incumbent on the wealthy or the Deputies to provide him with a monthly allowance for his subsistence. . . . By 'Deputies' is meant the representatives of the people, that is to say the members of the House of Justice." The prohibition against giving charity to people who beg does not preclude individuals and Spiritual Assemblies from extending financial assistance to the poor and needy or from providing them with opportunities to acquire such skills as would enable them to earn a livelihood. (The Universal House of Justice, in The Kitáb-i-Aqdas, p. 235)

Women and Work

So it will come to pass that when women participate fully and equally in the affairs of the world, when they enter confidently and capably the great arena of laws and politics, war will cease; for woman will be the obstacle and hindrance to it. This is true and without doubt.

138

It has been objected by some that woman is not equally capable with man and that she is deficient by creation. This is pure imagination. The difference in capability between man and woman is due entirely to opportunity and education. Heretofore woman has been denied the right and privilege of equal development. If equal opportunity be granted her, there is no doubt she would be the peer of man. ('Abdu'l-Bahá, *The Promulgation of Universal Peace*, pp. 186–87)

With regard to your question whether mothers should work outside the home, it is helpful to consider the matter from the perspective of the concept of a Bahá'í family. This concept is based on the principle that the man has primary responsibility for the financial support of the family, and the woman is the chief and primary educator of the children. This by no means implies that these functions are inflexibly fixed and cannot be changed and adjusted to suit particular family situations, nor does it mean that the place of the woman is confined to the home. Rather, while primary responsibility is assigned, it is anticipated that fathers would play a significant role in the education of the children and women could also be breadwinners. As you rightly indicated, 'Abdu'l-Bahá encouraged women to "participate fully and equally in the affairs of the world." (From a letter written on behalf of the Universal House of Justice, dated 9 August 1984, to an individual believer, in *Lights of Guidance*, no. 2118)

You ask about the admonition that everyone must work, and want to know if this means that you, a wife and mother, must work for a livelihood as your husband does. We are requested to enclose for your perusal an excerpt, "The twelfth Glad-Tidings," from Bahá'u'lláh's "Tablets of Bisharat." You will see that the directive is for the friends to be engaged in an occupation which will be of benefit to mankind. Home-making is a highly honourable and responsible work of fundamental importance for mankind. (From a letter written on behalf of the Universal House of Justice, dated 16 June 1982, in *Lights of Guidance*, no. 2117)

The effect of the persistent denial to women of full equality with men sharpens still further the challenge to science and religion in the economic life of humankind. To any objective observer the principle of the equality of the sexes is fundamental to all realistic thinking about the future well-being of the earth and its people. It represents a truth about human nature that has waited largely unrecognized throughout the long ages of the race's childhood and adolescence. "Women and men," is Bahá'u'lláh's emphatic assertion, "have been and will always be equal in the sight of God." The rational soul has no sex, and whatever social inequities may have been dictated by the survival requirements of the past, they clearly cannot be justified at a time when humanity stands at the threshold of maturity. A commitment to the establishment of full equality between men and women, in all departments of life and at every level of society, will be central to the success of efforts to conceive and implement a strategy of global development. (Bahá'í International Community, 16 July 1995, *The Prosperity of Humankind*)

Great emphasis is placed on education in the Bahá'í Faith as a means of promoting the advancement of women. The religion not only upholds the principle of universal education, but it accords priority to the education of girls and women when resources are limited, since it only through educated mothers that the benefits of knowledge can be most effectively and rapidly diffused throughout society. It advocates that girls and boys follow the same curriculum in school, and women are encouraged to study the arts, crafts, sciences and professions and to enter all fields of work, even those traditionally the exclusive province of men. (The Bahá'í International Community, "Religion as an Agent for Promoting the Advancement of Women at All Levels")

Preparing Children for Work
While the children are yet in their infancy feed them from the breast of heavenly grace, foster them in the cradle of all excellence, rear them in the embrace of bounty. Give them the advantage of every useful kind of knowl-

edge. Let them share in every new and rare and wondrous craft and art. Bring them up to work and strive, and accustom them to hardship. Teach them to dedicate their lives to matters of great import, and inspire them to undertake studies that will benefit mankind. ('Abdu'l-Bahá, *Selections from the Writings of 'Abdu'l-Bahá,* no. 102.3)

7

OBLIGATIONS OF WORLD LEADERS
TO PROMOTE JUSTICE AND PEACE

The government of the countries should conform to the Divine Law which gives equal justice to all.
This is the only way in which the deplorable superfluity of great wealth and miserable, demoralizing, degrading poverty can be abolished.
—'Abdu'l-Bahá, *Paris Talks,* no. 46.13

The Sacred Trust of Kings and Rulers

Lay not aside the fear of God, O kings of the earth, and beware that ye transgress not the bounds which the Almighty hath fixed. Observe the injunctions laid upon you in His Book, and take good heed not to overstep their limits. Be vigilant, that ye may not do injustice to anyone, be it to the extent of a grain of mustard seed. Tread ye the path of justice, for this, verily, is the straight path.

Compose your differences, and reduce your armaments, that the burden of your expenditures may be lightened, and that your minds and hearts may be tranquillized. Heal the dissensions that divide you, and ye will no longer be in need of any armaments except what the protection of your cities and territories demandeth. Fear ye God, and take heed not to outstrip the bounds of moderation, and be numbered among the extravagant.

We have learned that you are increasing your outlay every year, and are laying the burden thereof on your subjects. This, verily, is more than they can bear, and is a grievous injustice. Decide justly between men, and be ye the emblems of justice amongst them. This, if ye judge fairly, is the thing that behooveth you, and beseemeth your station.

Beware not to deal unjustly with any one that appealeth to you, and entereth beneath your shadow. Walk ye in the fear of God, and be ye of them that lead a godly life. Rest not on your power, your armies, and treasures. Put your whole trust and confidence in God, Who hath created you, and seek ye His help in all your affairs. Succor cometh from Him alone. He succoreth whom He will with the hosts of the heavens and of the earth.

Know ye that the poor are the trust of God in your midst. Watch that ye betray not His trust, that ye deal not unjustly with them and that ye walk not in the ways of the treacherous. Ye will most certainly be called upon to answer for His trust on the day when the Balance of Justice shall be set, the day when unto every one shall be rendered his due, when the doings of all men, be they rich or poor, shall be weighed.

If ye pay no heed unto the counsels which, in peerless and unequivocal language, We have revealed in this Tablet, Divine chastisement shall assail you from every direction, and the sentence of His justice shall be pronounced against you. On that day ye shall have no power to resist Him, and shall recognize your own impotence. Have mercy on yourselves and on those beneath you. Judge ye between them according to the precepts prescribed by God in His most holy and exalted Tablet, a Tablet wherein He hath assigned to each and every thing its settled measure, in which He hath given, with distinctness, an explanation of all things, and which is in itself a monition unto them that believe in Him. (Bahá'u'lláh, *Gleanings from the Writings of Bahá'u'lláh*, no. 143.1–6)

Know of a truth that your subjects are God's trust amongst you. Watch ye, therefore, over them as ye watch over your own selves. Beware that ye allow not wolves to become the shepherds of the fold, or pride and conceit to deter you from turning unto the poor and the desolate. (Bahá'u'lláh, *Epistle to the Son of the Wolf*, p. 53)

For is it not your clear duty to restrain the tyranny of the oppressor, and to deal equitably with your subjects, that your high sense of justice may be fully demonstrated to all mankind?

God hath committed into your hands the reins of the government of the people, that ye may rule with justice over them, safeguard the rights of the down-trodden, and punish the wrong-doers. If ye neglect the duty prescribed unto you by God in His Book, your names shall be numbered with those of the unjust in His sight. Grievous, indeed, will be your error. (Bahá'u'lláh, *Gleanings from the Writings of Bahá'u'lláh*, no. 141.2–3)

Place not thy reliance on thy treasures. Put thy whole confidence in the grace of God, thy Lord. Let Him be thy trust in whatever thou doest, and be of them that have submitted themselves to His Will. Let Him be thy helper and enrich thyself with His treasures, for with Him are the treasuries of the heavens and of the earth. He bestoweth them upon whom He will, and from whom He will He withholdeth them. There is none other God but Him, the All-Possessing, the All-Praised. All are but paupers at the door of His mercy; all are helpless before the revelation of His sovereignty, and beseech His favors.

Overstep not the bounds of moderation, and deal justly with them that serve thee. Bestow upon them according to their needs, and not to the extent that will enable them to lay up riches for themselves, to deck their persons, to embellish their homes, to acquire the things that are of no benefit unto them, and to be numbered with the extravagant. Deal with them with undeviating justice, so that none among them may either suffer want, or be pampered with luxuries. This is but manifest justice.

Allow not the abject to rule over and dominate them who are noble and worthy of honor, and suffer not the high-minded to be at the mercy of the contemptible and worthless, for this is what We observed upon Our arrival in the City (Constantinople), and to it We bear witness. We found among its inhabitants some who were possessed of an affluent fortune and lived in the midst of excessive riches, while others were in dire want and abject poverty. This ill beseemeth thy sovereignty, and is unworthy of thy rank.

Let My counsel be acceptable to thee, and strive thou to rule with equity among men, that God may exalt thy name and spread abroad the fame of thy justice in all the world. Beware lest thou aggrandize thy ministers at the expense of thy subjects. Fear the sighs of the poor and of the upright in heart who, at every break of day, bewail their plight, and be unto them a benignant sovereign. They, verily, are thy treasures on earth. It behooveth thee, therefore, to safeguard thy treasures from the assaults of them who wish to rob thee. Inquire into their affairs, and ascertain, every year, nay every month, their condition, and be not of them that are careless of their duty.

Set before thine eyes God's unerring Balance and, as one standing in His Presence, weigh in that Balance thine actions every day, every moment of thy life. Bring thyself to account ere thou art summoned to a reckoning, on the Day when no man shall have strength to stand for fear of God, the Day when the hearts of the heedless ones shall be made to tremble.

It behooveth every king to be as bountiful as the sun, which fostereth the growth of all beings, and giveth to each its due, whose benefits are not inherent in itself, but are ordained by Him Who is the Most Powerful, the Almighty. The king should be as generous, as liberal in his mercy as the clouds, the outpourings of whose bounty are showered upon every land, by the behest of Him Who is the Supreme Ordainer, the All-Knowing. (Bahá'u'lláh, *Gleanings from the Writings of Bahá'u'lláh*, no. 145.8–13)

The Great Being saith: O well-beloved ones! The tabernacle of unity hath been raised; regard ye not one another as strangers. Ye are the fruits of one tree, and the leaves of one branch. We cherish the hope that the light of justice may shine upon the world and sanctify it from tyranny. If the rulers and kings of the earth, the symbols of the power of God, exalted be His glory, arise and resolve to dedicate themselves to whatever will promote the highest interests of the whole of humanity, the reign of justice will assuredly be established amongst the children of men, and the effulgence of its light will envelop the whole earth. The Great Being saith: The structure of world stability and order hath been reared upon, and will continue to be sustained by, the twin pillars of reward and punishment. . . . Justice hath a mighty force at its command. It is none other than reward and punishment for the deeds of men. By the power of this force the tabernacle of order is established throughout the world, causing the wicked to restrain their natures for fear of punishment.

In another passage He hath written: Take heed, O concourse of the rulers of the world! There is no force on earth that can equal in its conquering power the force of justice and wisdom. I, verily, affirm that there is not, and hath never been, a host more mighty than that of justice and wisdom. Blessed is the king who marcheth with the ensign of wisdom unfurled before him, and the battalions of justice massed in his rear. He verily is the ornament that adorneth the brow of peace and the countenance of security. There can be no doubt whatever that if the daystar of justice, which the clouds of tyranny have obscured, were to shed its light upon men, the face of the earth would be completely transformed. (Bahá'u'lláh, *Tablets of Bahá'u'lláh*, pp. 164–65)

O ye rulers of the earth! Wherefore have ye clouded the radiance of the Sun, and caused it to cease from shining? Hearken unto the counsel given you by the Pen of the Most High, that haply both ye and the poor may attain unto tranquility and peace. We beseech God to assist the kings of the earth to establish peace on earth. He, verily, doth what He willeth.

O kings of the earth! We see you increasing every year your expenditures, and laying the burden thereof on your subjects. This, verily, is wholly and grossly unjust. Fear the sighs and tears of this wronged One, and lay not excessive burdens on your peoples. Do not rob them to rear palaces for yourselves; nay rather choose for them that which ye choose for yourselves. Thus We unfold to your eyes that which profiteth you, if ye but perceive. Your people are your treasures. Beware lest your rule violate the commandments of God, and ye deliver your wards to the hands of the robber. By them ye rule, by their means ye subsist, by their aid ye conquer. Yet, how disdainfully ye look upon them! How strange, how very strange! (Bahá'u'lláh, *Gleanings from the Writings of Bahá'u'lláh*, no. 119.1–2)

Beseech ye the True One—glorified be His Name—that He may graciously shield the manifestations of dominion and power from the suggestions of self and desire and shed the radiance of justice and guidance upon them. (Bahá'u'lláh, *Tablets of Bahá'u'lláh*, p. 65)

The faults of kings, like their favors, can be great. A king who is not deterred by the vainglory of power and authority from observing justice, nor is deprived of the splendors of the daystar of equity by luxury, riches, glory or the marshalling of hosts and legions shall occupy a high rank and a sublime station amongst the Concourse on high. It is incumbent upon everyone to extend aid and to manifest kindness to so noble a soul. Well is it with the king who keepeth a tight hold on the reins of his passion, restraineth his anger and preferreth justice and fairness to injustice and tyranny. (Bahá'u'lláh, *Tablets of Bahá'u'lláh*, p. 65)

O rulers of the earth! Be reconciled among yourselves, that ye may need no more armaments save in a measure to safeguard your territories and dominions. Beware lest ye disregard the counsel of the All-Knowing, the Faithful.

Be united, O kings of the earth, for thereby will the tempest of discord be stilled amongst you, and your peoples find rest, if ye be of them that comprehend. Should any one among you take up arms against another, rise ye all against him, for this is naught but manifest justice. (Bahá'u'lláh, *Gleanings from the Writings of Bahá'u'lláh*, no. 119.4–5)

Shouldst thou cause rivers of justice to spread their waters amongst thy subjects, God would surely aid thee with the hosts of the unseen and of the seen, and would strengthen thee in thine affairs. No God is there but Him. All creation and its empire are His. Unto Him return the works of the faithful. (Bahá'u'lláh, *Gleanings from the Writings of Bahá'u'lláh,* no. 114.6)

It is incumbent upon everyone to aid those dayprings of authority and sources of command who are adorned with the ornament of equity and justice. (Bahá'u'lláh, *Tablets of Bahá'u'lláh,* p. 221)

The just king is the shadow of God in the earth; all should take refuge under the shadow of his justice and rest in the shade of his favor. ('Abdu'l-Bahá, *A Traveler's Narrative,* p. 65)

That which befits the kingly dignity and beseems the world-ordering diadem is this, that all subjects of every class and creed should be the objects of bounty, and [should abide] in the utmost tranquility and prosperity under the wide shadow of the King's justice. For the divine shadow is the refuge of all the dwellers upon earth and the asylum of all mankind; it is not limited to one party. ('Abdu'l-Bahá, *A Traveler's Narrative,* p. 86)

Kings must rule with wisdom and justice; prince, peer and peasant alike have equal rights to just treatment, there must be no favor shown to individuals. A judge must be no "respecter of persons," but must administer the law with strict impartiality in every case brought before him. ('Abdu'l-Bahá, *Paris Talks,* no. 47.4)

The Character, Conduct, and Obligations of Elected Representatives of the People

While the setting up of parliaments, the organizing of assemblies of consultation, constitutes the very foundation and bedrock of government, there are several essential requirements which these institutions must fulfill. First, the elected members must be righteous, God-fearing, high-minded, incorruptible. Second, they must be fully cognizant, in every particular, of the laws of God, informed as to the highest principles of law, versed in the rules which govern the management of internal affairs and the conduct of emoluments.

Let it not be imagined that members of this type would be impossible to find. Through the grace of God and His chosen ones, and the high endeavors of the devoted and the consecrated, every difficulty can be easily resolved, every problem however complex will prove simpler than blinking an eye.

If, however, the members of these consultative assemblies are inferior, ignorant, uninformed of the laws of government and administration, unwise, of low aim, indifferent, idle, self-seeking, no benefit will accrue from the organizing of such bodies. Where, in the past, if a poor man wanted his rights he had only to offer a gift to one individual, now he would either have to renounce all hope of justice or else satisfy the entire membership. ('Abdu'l-Bahá, *The Secret of Divine Civilization,* ¶31–33)

Those persons who are selected to serve the public, or are appointed to administrative positions, should perform their duties in a spirit of true servitude and ready compliance. That is to say they should be distinguished by their goodly disposition and virtuous character, content themselves with their allotted remuneration and act with trustworthiness in all their doings. They should keep themselves aloof from unworthy motives and be far removed above covetous design; for rectitude, probity and righteousness are among the most potent means of attracting the grace of God and securing both the prosperity of the country and the welfare of the people. Glory and honour for man are not to be found in fortunes and riches, least of all in those which have been unlawfully amassed though extortion, embezzlement and corruption practiced at the expense of an exploited populace. Supreme honour, nobility and greatness in the human world, and true fidelity in this life and the life to come—all consist in equality and righteousness, sanctity and detachment. If a man would seek distinction he should suffice himself with a frugal provision, seek to better the lot of the realm, choose the way of justice and fair mindedness, and tread the path of high-spirited service. Such a one, needy though he be, shall win imperishable riches and attain unto everlasting honour. ('Abdu'l-Bahá, in *Lights of Guidance*, no. 1473)

If bribery and corruption, known today by the pleasant names of gifts and favors, were forever excluded, would this threaten the foundations of justice? ('Abdu'l-Bahá, *The Secret of Divine Civilization*, ¶27)

How foolish and ignorant must a man be, how base his nature, and how vile the clay of which he is fashioned, if he would defile himself with the contamination of bribery, corruption and perfidy towards the state! Truly, the vermin of the earth are to be preferred to such people! ('Abdu'l-Bahá, from a Tablet translated from the Persian, in *The Compilation of Compilations*, vol. II, no. 2073)

There are spiritual principles, or what some call human values, by which solutions can be found for every social problem. Any well-intentioned group can in a general sense devise practical solutions to its problems, but good intentions and practical knowledge are usually not enough. The essential merit of spiritual principle is that it not only presents a perspective which harmonizes with that which is immanent in human nature, it also induces an attitude, a dynamic, a will, an aspiration, which facilitate the discovery and implementation of practical measures. Leaders of governments and all in authority would be well served in their efforts to solve problems if they would first seek to identify the principles involved and then be guided by them. (The Universal House of Justice, *The Promise of World Peace*, ¶37)

Above all else, leaders for the next generation must be motivated by a sincere desire to serve the entire community and must understand that leadership is a responsibility; not a path to privilege. For too long, leadership has been understood, by both leaders and followers, as the assertion of control over others. Indeed, this age demands a new definition of leadership and a new type of leader.

This is especially true in the international arena. In order to establish a sense of trust, win the confidence, and inculcate a fond affinity in the hearts of the world's people for institutions of the international order, these leaders will have to reflect on their own actions.

Through an unblemished record of personal integrity, they must help restore confidence and trust in government. They must embody the characteristics of honesty, humility and sincerity of purpose in seeking the truth of a situation. They must be committed to and guided by principles, thereby acting in the best long-term interests of humanity as a whole.

"Let your vision be world-embracing, rather than confined to your own selves," Bahá'u'lláh wrote. "Do not busy yourselves in your own concerns; let your thoughts be fixed upon that which will rehabilitate the fortunes of mankind and sanctify the hearts and souls of men." (Bahá'í International Community, *Turning Point For All Nations*)

The institutions of society will succeed in eliciting and directing the potentialities latent in the consciousness of the world's peoples to the extent that the exercise of authority is governed by principles that are in harmony with the evolving interests of a rapidly maturing human race. Such principles include the obligation of those in authority to win the confidence, respect, and genuine support of those whose actions they seek to govern; to consult openly and to the fullest extent possible with all whose interests are affected by decisions being arrived at; to assess in an objective manner both the real needs and the aspirations of the communities they serve; to benefit from scientific and moral advancement in order to make appropriate use of the community's resources, including the energies of its members. No single principle of effective authority is so important as giving priority to building and maintaining unity among the members of a society and the members of its administrative institutions. Reference has already been made to the intimately associated issue of commitment to the search for justice in all matters.

Clearly, such principles can operate only within a culture that is essentially democratic in spirit and method. To say this, however, is not to endorse the ideology of partisanship that has everywhere boldly assumed democra-cy's name and which, despite impressive contributions to human progress in the past, today finds itself mired in the cynicism, apathy, and corruption to which it has given rise. In selecting those who are to take collective decisions on its behalf, society does not need and is not well served by the political theater of nominations, candidature, electioneering, and solicitation. It lies within the capacity of all people, as they become progressively educated and convinced that their real development interests are being served by programs proposed to them, to adopt electoral procedures that will gradually refine the selection of their decision-making bodies.

As the integration of humanity gains momentum, those who are thus selected will increasingly have to see all their efforts in a global perspective. Not only at the national, but also at the local level, the elected governors of human affairs should, in Bahá'u'lláh's view, consider themselves responsible for the welfare of all of humankind. (Bahá'í International Community, *The Prosperity of Humankind*)

The question of poverty places particular responsibility on elected leaders and their governments. While some have argued that poverty itself leads to poor governance, causality often moves in the opposite direction: better governance leads to better development outcomes. Central to the issue of governance is the inescapable question of character—the values that a leader brings to his or her office largely define the direction and fruits of his or her work. Trustworthiness is foremost among these, as it fosters credibility with the public and with other leaders, builds support for government initiatives and engenders stability and security. Effective leaders must not only exercise an impeccable ethic but also work to strengthen the character of the nation's economic, social, legal and educational institutions, to improve the regula-tory framework, and to manage scarce resources effectively. Where earnings are concerned, they must be content with a lawful and modest remuneration. As the substance of politics becomes increasingly global, elected leaders must show the vision and the courage to gradually align national interests with the requirements of the evolving global community. (Bahá'í International Community, "Eradicating Poverty: Moving Forward as One")

Appointing Trustworthy Ministers of State

Governments should fully acquaint themselves with the conditions of those they govern, and confer upon them positions according to desert and merit. It is enjoined upon every ruler and sovereign to consider this matter with the utmost care that the traitor may not usurp the position of the faithful, nor the despoiler rule in the place of the trustworthy. (Bahá'u'lláh, *Tablets of Bahá'u'lláh*, p. 127)

Take heed that thou resign not the reins of the affairs of thy state into the hands of others, and repose not thy confidence in ministers unworthy of thy trust, and be not of them that live in heedlessness. Shun them whose hearts are turned away from thee, and place not thy confidence in them, and entrust them not with thy affairs and the affairs of such as profess thy faith. Beware that thou allow not the wolf to become the shepherd of God's flock, and surrender not the fate of His loved ones to the mercy of the malicious. Expect not that they who violate the ordinances of God will be trustworthy or sincere in the faith they profess. Avoid them, and preserve strict guard over thyself, lest their devices and mischief hurt thee. Turn away from them, and fix thy gaze upon God, thy Lord, the All-Glorious, the Most Bountiful. He that giveth up himself wholly to God, God shall, assuredly, be with him; and he that placeth his complete trust in God, God shall, verily, protect him from whatsoever may harm him, and shield him from the wickedness of every evil plotter. (Bahá'u'lláh, *Gleanings from the Writings of Bahá'u'lláh*, no. 114.4)

Have a care not to entrust thine affairs of state entirely into another's hands. None can discharge thy functions better than thine own self. Thus do We make clear unto thee Our words of wisdom, and send down upon thee that which can enable thee to pass over from the left hand of oppression to the right hand of justice, and approach the resplendent ocean of His favors. Such is the path which the kings that were before thee have trodden, they that acted equitably towards their subjects, and walked in the ways of unde-viating justice. (Bahá'u'lláh, *Gleanings from the Writings of Bahá'u'lláh*, no. 114.14)

Beware, O King, that thou gather not around thee such ministers as follow the desires of a corrupt inclination, as have cast behind their backs that which hath been committed into their hands and manifestly betrayed their trust. Be bounteous to others as God hath been bounteous to thee, and abandon not the interests of thy people to the mercy of such ministers as these. Lay not aside the fear of God, and be thou of them that act uprightly. Gather around thee those ministers from whom thou canst perceive the fragrance of faith and of justice, and take thou counsel with them, and choose whatever is best in thy sight, and be of them that act generously. (Bahá'u'lláh, *Gleanings from the Writings of Bahá'u'lláh*, no. 114.2)

We have also heard that thou hast entrusted the reins of counsel into the hands of the representatives of the people. Thou, indeed, hast done well, for thereby the foundations of the edifice of thine affairs will be strengthened, and the hearts of all that are beneath thy shadow, whether high or low, will be tranquillized. It behooveth them, however, to be trustworthy among His servants, and to regard themselves as the representatives of all that dwell on earth. This is what counselleth them, in this Tablet, He Who is the Ruler, the All-Wise. . . . Blessed is he that entereth the assembly for the sake of God, and judgeth between men with pure justice. He, indeed, is of the blissful. (Bahá'u'lláh, *Epistle to the Son of the Wolf,* p. 61)

When a ruler knows that his judgments will be weighed in a balance by the Divine Judge, and that if he be not found wanting he will come into the Celestial Kingdom and that the light of the Heavenly Bounty will shine upon him, then will he surely act with justice and equity. Behold how important it is that Ministers of State should be enlightened by religion! ('Abdu'l-Bahá, *Paris Talks*, no. 49.8)

If administrators of the law would take into consideration the spiritual consequences of their decisions, and follow the guidance of religion, "They would be Divine agents in the world of action, the representatives of God for those who are on earth, and they would defend, for the love of God, the interests of His servants as they would defend their own." If a governor realizes his responsibility, and fears to defy the Divine Law, his judgments will be just. Above all, if he believes that the consequences of his actions will follow him beyond his earthly life, and that "as he sows so must he reap," such a man will surely avoid injustice and tyranny. ('Abdu'l-Bahá, *Paris Talks*, no. 49.6)

To the Rulers of America

Hearken ye, O Rulers of America and the Presidents of the Republics therein, unto that which the Dove is warbling on the Branch of Eternity: There is none other God but Me, the Ever-Abiding, the Forgiving, the All-Bountiful. Adorn ye the temple of dominion with the ornament of justice and of the fear of God, and its head with the crown of the remembrance of your Lord, the Creator of the heavens. Thus counseleth you He Who is the Dayspring of Names, as bidden by Him Who is the All-Knowing, the All-Wise. The Promised One hath appeared in this glorified Station, whereat all beings, both seen and unseen, have rejoiced. Take ye advantage of the Day of God. Verily, to meet Him is better for you than all that whereon the sun shineth, could ye but know it. O concourse of rulers! Give ear unto that which hath been raised from the Dayspring of Grandeur: Verily, there is none other God but Me, the Lord of Utterance, the All-Knowing. Bind ye the broken with the hands of justice, and crush the oppressor who flourisheth with the rod of the commandments of your Lord, the Ordainer, the All-Wise. (Bahá'u'lláh, The Kitáb-i-Aqdas, ¶88)

More specifically has the Author of the Bahá'í Revelation Himself chosen to confer upon the rulers of the American continent the unique honor of addressing them collectively in the Kitáb-i-Aqdas, His most Holy Book, significantly exhorting them to "adorn the temple of dominion with the ornament of justice and of the fear of God, and its head with the crown of the remembrance" of their Lord, and bidding them "bind with the hands of justice the broken," and "crush the oppressor" with the "rod of the commandments" of their "Lord, the Ordainer, the All-Wise." "The continent of America," wrote 'Abdu'l-Bahá, "is, in the eyes of the one true God, the land wherein the splendors of His light shall be revealed, where the mysteries of His Faith shall be unveiled, where the righteous will abide and the free assemble." "The American continent," He has furthermore predicted, "giveth signs and evidences of very great advancement. Its future is even more promising, for its influence and illumination are far reaching. It will lead all nations spiritually." (Shoghi Effendi, *God Passes By*, pp. 400–1)

The Role of Religious Leaders

O Supreme Pontiff! Incline thine ear unto that which the Fashioner of moldering bones counselleth thee, as voiced by Him Who is His Most Great Name. Sell all the embellished ornaments thou dost possess, and expend them in the path of God, Who causeth the night to return upon the day, and the day to return upon the night. Abandon thy kingdom unto the kings, and emerge from thy habitation, with thy face set towards the Kingdom, and, detached from the world, then speak forth the praises of thy Lord betwixt earth and heaven. Thus hath bidden thee He Who is the Possessor of Names, on the part of thy Lord, the Almighty, the All-Knowing. Exhort thou the kings and say: "Deal equitably with men. Beware lest ye transgress the bounds fixed in the Book." This indeed becometh thee. Beware lest thou appropriate unto thyself the things of the world and the riches thereof. Leave them unto such as desire them, and cleave unto that which hath been enjoined upon thee by Him Who is the Lord of creation. Should any one offer thee all the treasures of the earth, refuse to even glance upon them. Be as thy Lord hath been. (Bahá'u'lláh, *The Summons of the Lord of Hosts*, no. 1.118)

Our hope is that the world's religious leaders and the rulers thereof will unitedly arise for the reformation of this age and the rehabilitation of its fortunes. Let them, after meditating on its needs, take counsel together and, through anxious and full deliberation, administer to a diseased and sorely-afflicted world the remedy it requireth. . . . It is incumbent upon them who are in authority to exercise moderation in all things. Whatsoever passeth beyond the limits of moderation will cease to exert a beneficial influence. Consider for instance such things as liberty, civilization and the like. However much men of understanding may favorably regard them, they will, if carried to excess, exercise a pernicious influence upon men. . . . Please God, the peoples of the world may be led, as the result of the high endeavors exerted by their rulers and the wise and learned amongst men, to recognize their best interests. How long will humanity persist in its waywardness? How long will injustice continue? How long is chaos and confusion to reign amongst men? How long will discord agitate the face of society? . . . The winds of despair are, alas, blowing from every direction, and the strife that divideth and afflicteth the human race is daily increasing. The signs of impending convulsions and chaos can now be discerned, inasmuch as the prevailing order appeareth to be lamentably defective. I beseech God, exalted be His glory, that He may graciously awaken the peoples of the earth, may grant that the end of their conduct may be profitable unto them, and aid them to accomplish that which beseemeth their station. (Bahá'u'lláh, *Gleanings from the Writings of Bahá'u'lláh*, no. 110.1)

Politics are occupied with the material things of life. Religious teachers should not invade the realm of politics; they should concern themselves with the spiritual education of the people; they should ever give good counsel to men, trying to serve God and human kind; they should endeavor to awaken spiritual aspiration, and strive to enlarge the understanding and knowledge of humanity, to improve morals, and to increase the love for justice. ('Abdu'l-Bahá, *Paris Talks,* no. 49.11)

Religious strife, throughout history, has been the cause of innumerable wars and conflicts, a major blight to progress, and is increasingly abhorrent to the people of all faiths and no faith. Followers of all religions must be willing to face the basic questions which this strife raises, and to arrive at clear answers. How are the differences between them to be resolved, both in theory and in practice? The challenge facing the religious leaders of mankind is to contemplate, with hearts filled with the spirit of compassion and a desire for truth, the plight of humanity, and to ask themselves whether they cannot, in humility before their Almighty Creator, submerge their theological differences in a great spirit of mutual forbearance that will enable them to work together for the advancement of human understanding and peace. (The Universal House of Justice, *The Promise of World Peace,* ¶32)

8

ADVANCING ECONOMIC JUSTICE AT THE GRASSROOTS LEVEL

The amelioration of the conditions of the world requires the reconstruction of human society and efforts to improve the material well-being of humanity. The Bahá'í approach to this task is evolutionary and multifaceted, involving not only the spiritual transformation of individuals but the establishment of an administrative system based on the application of justice, a system which is at once the 'nucleus' and the 'pattern' of the future World Order, together with the implementation of programmes of social and economic development that derive their impetus from the grass roots of the community.
—The Universal House of Justice, *Messages 1963 to 1986*, no. 425.8

Worldwide Bahá'í Community Engagement in Social and Economic Development

Passivity is bred by the forces of society today. A desire to be entertained is nurtured from childhood, with increasing efficiency, cultivating generations willing to be led by whoever proves skillful at appealing to superficial emotions. Even in many educational systems students are treated as though they were receptacles designed to receive information. That the Bahá'í world has succeeded in developing a culture which promotes a way of thinking, studying, and acting, in which all consider themselves as treading a common path of service—supporting one another and advancing together, respectful of the knowledge that each one possesses at any given moment and avoiding the tendency to divide the believers into categories such as deepened and

161

uninformed—is an accomplishment of enormous proportions. And therein lie the dynamics of an irrepressible movement. (The Universal House of Justice, Riḍván 2010, to the Bahá'ís of the world)

In our Riḍván 2008 message we indicated that, as the friends continued to labour at the level of the cluster, they would find themselves drawn further and further into the life of society and would be challenged to extend the process of systematic learning in which they are engaged to encompass a widening range of human endeavours. A rich tapestry of community life begins to emerge in every cluster as acts of communal worship, interspersed with discussions undertaken in the intimate setting of the home, are woven together with activities that provide spiritual education to all members of the population—adults, youth and children. Social consciousness is heightened naturally as, for example, lively conversations proliferate among parents regarding the aspirations of their children and service projects spring up at the initiative of junior youth. Once human resources in a cluster are in sufficient abundance, and the pattern of growth firmly established, the community's engagement with society can, and indeed must, increase. At this crucial point in the unfoldment of the Plan, when so many clusters are nearing such a stage, it seems appropriate that the friends everywhere would reflect on the nature of the contributions which their growing, vibrant communities will make to the material and spiritual progress of society. In this respect, it will prove fruitful to think in terms of two interconnected, mutually reinforcing areas of activity: involvement in social action and participation in the prevalent discourses of society.

Over the decades, the Bahá'í community has gained much experience in these two areas of endeavour. There are, of course, a great many Bahá'ís who are engaged as individuals in social action and public discourse through their occupations. A number of non-governmental organizations, inspired by the teachings of the Faith and operating at the regional and national levels, are working in the field of social and economic development for the betterment of their people. Agencies of National Spiritual Assemblies are contributing through various avenues to the promotion of ideas conducive to public welfare. At the international level, agencies such as the United Nations Office of the Bahá'í International Community are performing a similar function. To the extent necessary and desirable, the friends working at the grassroots of the community will draw on this experience and capacity as they strive to address the concerns of the society around them.

Most appropriately conceived in terms of a spectrum, social action can range from fairly informal efforts of limited duration undertaken by individuals or small groups of friends to programmes of social and economic development with a high level of complexity and sophistication implemented by Bahá'í-inspired organizations. Irrespective of its scope and scale, all social action seeks to apply the teachings and principles of the Faith to improve some aspect of the social or economic life of a population, however modestly. Such endeavours are distinguished, then, by their stated purpose to promote the material well-being of the population, in addition to its spiritual welfare. That the world civilization now on humanity's horizon must achieve a dynamic coherence between the material and spiritual requirements of life is central to the Bahá'í teachings. Clearly this ideal has profound implications for the nature of any social action pursued by Bahá'ís, whatever its scope and range of influence. Though conditions will vary from country to country, and perhaps from cluster to cluster, eliciting from the friends a variety of endeavours, there are certain fundamental concepts that all should bear in mind. One is the centrality of knowledge to social existence. The perpetuation of ignorance is a most grievous form of oppression; it reinforces the many walls of prejudice that stand as barriers to the realization of the oneness of humankind, at once the goal and operating principle of Bahá'u'lláh's Revelation. Access to knowledge is the right of every human being, and participation in its generation, application and diffusion a responsibility that all must shoulder in the great enterprise of building a prosperous world civilization—each individual according to his or her talents and abilities. Justice demands universal participation. Thus, while social action may involve the provision of goods and services in some form, its primary concern must be to build capacity within a given population to participate in creating a better world. Social change is not a project that one group of people carries out for the benefit of another. The scope and complexity of social action must be commensurate with the human resources available in a village or neighbourhood to carry it forward. Efforts best begin, then, on a modest scale and grow organically as capacity within the population develops. Capacity rises to new levels, of course, as the protagonists of social change learn to apply with increasing effectiveness elements of Bahá'u'lláh's Revelation, together with the contents and methods of science, to their social reality. This reality they must strive to read in a manner consistent with His teachings—seeing in their fellow human beings gems of inestimable value and recognizing the effects of the dual process of integration and disintegration on both hearts and minds, as well as on social structures.

Effective social action serves to enrich participation in the discourses of society, just as the insights gained from engaging in certain discourses can help to clarify the concepts that shape social action. At the level of the cluster, involvement in public discourse can range from an act as simple as introducing Bahá'í ideas into everyday conversation to more formal activities such as the preparation of articles and attendance at gatherings, dedicated to themes of social concern—climate change and the environment, governance and human rights, to mention a few. It entails, as well, meaningful interactions with civic groups and local organizations in villages and neighbourhoods.

In this connection, we feel compelled to raise a warning: It will be important for all to recognize that the value of engaging in social action and public discourse is not to be judged by the ability to bring enrolments. Though endeavours in these two areas of activity may well effect an increase in the size of the Bahá'í community, they are not undertaken for this purpose. Sincerity in this respect is an imperative. Moreover, care should be exercised to avoid overstating the Bahá'í experience or drawing undue attention to fledgling efforts, such as the junior youth spiritual empowerment programme, which are best left to mature at their own pace. The watchword in all cases is humility. While conveying enthusiasm about their beliefs, the friends should guard against projecting an air of triumphalism, hardly appropriate among themselves, much less in other circumstances.

In describing for you these new opportunities now opening at the level of the cluster, we are not asking you to alter in any way your current course. Nor should it be imagined that such opportunities represent an alternative arena of service, competing with the expansion and consolidation work for the community's limited resources and energies. Over the coming year, the institute process and the pattern of activity that it engenders should continue to be strengthened, and teaching should remain uppermost in the mind of every believer. Further involvement in the life of society should not be sought prematurely. It will proceed naturally as the friends in every cluster persevere in applying the provisions of the Plan through a process of action, reflection, consultation and study, and learn as a result. Involvement in the life of society will flourish as the capacity of the community to promote its own growth and to maintain its vitality is gradually raised. It will achieve coherence with efforts to expand and consolidate the community to the extent that it draws on elements of the conceptual framework which governs the current series of global Plans. And it will contribute to the movement of populations towards Bahá'u'lláh's vision of a prosperous and peaceful world civilization to the degree that it employs these elements creatively in new areas of learning. (The Universal House of Justice, Riḍván 2010, to the Bahá'ís of the world)

The coming global endeavor to which the friends will be summoned calls for the application of proven strategies, systematic action, informed analysis, and keen insight. Yet above all, it is a spiritual enterprise, and its true character should never be obscured. The urgency to act is impelled by the world's desperate condition. All that the followers of Bahá'u'lláh have learned in the last twenty years must culminate in the accomplishments of the next five. The scale of what is being asked of them brings to mind one of His Tablets in which He describes, in striking terms, the challenge entailed in spreading His Cause:

How many the lands that remained untilled and uncultivated; and how many the lands that were tilled and cultivated, and yet remained without water; and how many the lands which, when the harvest time arrived, no harvester came forth to reap! However, through the wonders of God's favor and the revelations of His loving-kindness, We cherish the hope that souls may appear who are the embodiments of heavenly virtue and who will occupy themselves with teaching the Cause of God and training all that dwell on earth. (The Universal House of Justice, letter dated 29 December 2015, to the Conference of the Continental Boards of Counselors)

A natural outcome of the rise both in resources and in consciousness of the implications of the Revelation for the life of a population is the stirrings of social action. Not infrequently, initiatives of this kind emerge organically out of the junior youth spiritual empowerment programme or are prompted by consultations about local conditions that occur at community gatherings. The forms that such endeavours can assume are diverse and include, for example, tutorial assistance to children, projects to better the physical environment, and activities to improve health and prevent disease. Some initiatives become sustained and gradually grow. In various places the founding of a community school at the grassroots has arisen from a heightened concern for the proper education of children and awareness of its importance, flowing naturally from the study of institute materials. On occasion, the efforts of the friends can be greatly reinforced through the work of an established Bahá'í-inspired organization functioning in the vicinity. However humble an instance of social action might be at the beginning, it is an indication of a people cultivating within themselves a critical capacity, one that holds infinite potential and significance for the centuries ahead: learning how to apply the Revelation to the manifold dimensions of social existence. All such initiatives also serve to enrich participation, at an individual and collective level, in prevalent discourses of the wider community. As expected, the friends are being drawn further into the life of society—a development which is inherent in the pattern of action in a cluster from the very start, but which is now much more pronounced.

For the movement of a population to have come this far demonstrates that the process which brought it about is strong enough to achieve and sustain a high degree of participation in all aspects of the capacity-building endeavour and manage the complexity entailed. This is another milestone for the friends to pass, the third in succession since the process of growth in a cluster was begun. It denotes the appearance of a system for extending, in centre after centre, a dynamic pattern of community life that can engage a people—men and women, youth and adults—in the work of their own spiritual and social transformation. This has already come about in around two hundred clusters, covering a range of socio-economic circumstances, and we anticipate that, by the conclusion of the coming Plan, it will be observable in several hundred more. It is a future to which the friends labouring in thousands of clusters elsewhere can aspire.

In some of the clusters where growth has advanced to this extent, an even more thrilling development has occurred. There are locations within these clusters where a significant percentage of the entire population is now involved in community-building activities. For instance, there are small villages where the institute has been able to engage the participation of all the children and junior youth in its programmes. When the reach of activity is extensive, the societal impact of the Faith becomes more evident. The Bahá'í community is afforded higher standing as a distinctive moral voice in the life of a people and is able to contribute an informed perspective to the discourses around it on, say, the development of the younger generations. Figures of authority from the wider society start to draw on the insight and experience arising from initiatives of social action inspired by Bahá'u'lláh's teachings. Conversations influenced by those teachings, concerned with the common weal, permeate an ever-broader cross section of the population, to the point where an effect on the general discourse in a locality can be perceived. Beyond the Bahá'í community, people are coming to regard the

Local Spiritual Assembly as a radiant source of wisdom to which they too can turn for illumination.

We recognize that developments like these are yet a distant prospect for many, even in clusters where the pattern of activity embraces large numbers. But in some places, this is the work of the moment. In such clusters, while the friends continue to be occupied with sustaining the process of growth, other dimensions of Bahá'í endeavour claim an increasing share of their attention. They are seeking to understand how a flourishing local population can transform the society of which it is an integral part. This will be a new frontier of learning for the foreseeable future, where insights will be generated that will ultimately benefit the whole Bahá'í world. (The Universal House of Justice, letter dated 29 December 2015, to the Conference of the Continental Boards of Counselors)

Bahá'í activity in the field of social and economic development seeks to promote the well-being of people of all walks of life, whatever their beliefs or background. It represents the efforts of the Bahá'í community to effect constructive social change, as it learns to apply the teachings of the Faith, together with knowledge accumulated in different fields of human endeavour, to social reality. Its purpose is neither to proclaim the Cause nor to serve as a vehicle for conversion. (*Social Action*, A paper prepared by the Office of Social and Economic Development at the Bahá'í World Center, 26 November 2012)

In its Riḍván 2010 message, the Universal House of Justice called on the Bahá'ís of the world to reflect on the contributions that their growing, vibrant communities will make to the material and spiritual progress of society. In this connection, the House of Justice made reference to the process of community building set in motion in so many clusters across the globe by the core activities associated with the current series of global Plans. "A rich tapestry of community life," it was noted, "begins to emerge in every cluster as acts of communal worship, interspersed with discussions undertaken in the intimate setting of the home, are woven together with activities that provide spiritual education to all members of the population—adults, youth and children." "Social consciousness is heightened naturally as, for example," the message went on to explain, "lively conversations proliferate among parents regarding the aspirations of their children and service projects spring up at the initiative of junior youth." The House of Justice then made the following statement: "Once human resources in a cluster are in sufficient abundance, and the pattern of growth firmly established, the community's engagement with society can, and indeed must, increase." Later in the same message, the House of Justice defined the sphere of social action in these terms:

> Most appropriately conceived in terms of a spectrum, social action can range from fairly informal efforts of limited duration undertaken by individuals or small groups of friends to programmes of social and economic development with a high level of complexity and sophistication implemented by Bahá'í-inspired organizations. Irrespective of its scope and scale, all social action seeks to apply the teachings and principles of the Faith to improve some aspect of the social or economic life of a population, however modestly.

To contribute to discussions under way at all levels of the Bahá'í community about the nature of its involvement in social action, we have prepared this paper on the basis of experience gained over the years in the area of social and economic development. The insights presented are drawn from relatively complex development endeavours, yet they shed light on the character of initiatives across the entire spectrum, as all instances of social action, irrespective of size, rely on a shared set of concepts, principles, methods, and approaches. (*Social Action*, A paper prepared by the Office of Social and Economic Development at the Bahá'í World Center, 26 November 2012)

The mode of operation adopted in the area of social and economic development, in common with other areas of Bahá'í activity, is one of learning in action. When efforts are carried out in a learning mode—characterized by constant action, reflection, consultation, and study—visions and strategies are re-examined time and again. As tasks are accomplished, obstacles removed, resources multiplied, and lessons learned, modifications are made in goals and methods. The learning process, which is given direction through appropriate institutional arrangements, unfolds in a way that resembles the growth and differentiation of a living organism. Haphazard change is avoided, and continuity of action maintained.

On several occasions, the Universal House of Justice, referring to the way in which those serving at the level of the cluster will be drawn further and further into the life of society, has indicated: "In the approaches you take, the methods you adopt, and the instruments you employ, you will need to achieve the same degree of coherence that characterizes the pattern of growth presently under way." How the first stirrings in the area of social action will manifest themselves in cluster after cluster where the dual process of expansion and consolidation is robust, the extent to which cultivation and direction from the institutions will be required, and the ways in which endeavours of social action will strengthen the fabric of community life— these are among the issues that will be the subject of an increasingly intense process of learning in the coming years.

Achieving progressively higher degrees of coherence both within and among the broad interconnected fields of endeavour in which the Bahá'í community is engaged is clearly a vital concern. It suggests that areas of activity are to be complementary, integrated, and mutually supportive. Further, it implies the existence of a common, overarching framework that gives shape to activities and which evolves and becomes more elaborate as experience accumulates. (*Social Action*, A paper prepared by the Office of Social and Economic Development at the Bahá'í World Center, 26 November 2012)

The Building of Capacity
When development is seen in terms of the participation of more and more people in a collective process of learning, then the concept of capacity build-

ing assumes particular importance. Thus, while any instance of social action would naturally aim at improving some aspect of the life of a population, it cannot focus simply on the provision of goods and services—an approach to development so prevalent in the world today, one which often carries with it attitudes of paternalism and which employs methods that disempower those who should be the protagonists of change. Setting and achieving specific goals to improve conditions is a legitimate concern of social action; yet, far more essential is the accompanying rise in the capacity of the participants in an endeavour to contribute to progress. Of course, the imperative to build capacity is not only relevant to the individual, important though that may be; it is equally applicable to institutions and the community, the other two protagonists in the advancement of civilization.

At the level of the individual, the influence of the training institute is vital. As it helps to equip individuals with the spiritual insights and knowledge, the qualities and attitudes, and the skills and abilities needed to carry out acts of service integral to Bahá'í community life, the institute creates a pool of human resources that makes it possible for endeavours of social and economic development to flourish. The participants in such endeavours are able to acquire, in turn, knowledge and skills pertinent to the specific areas of action in which they are engaged—health, agricultural production, and education, to name but a few—while continuing to strengthen those capacities already cultivated by the institute, for instance, fostering unity in diversity, promoting justice, participating effectively in consultation, and accompanying others in their efforts to serve humanity.

Similarly, the question of institutional capacity requires due attention. As the institutions of the Faith gain experience, particularly in the context of their efforts to ensure that the provisions of the global Plans are met, they become increasingly adept at offering assistance, resources, encouragement, and loving guidance to appropriate initiatives; at consulting freely and harmoniously among themselves and with people they serve; and at channelling individual and collective energies towards the transformation of society. So, too, must every effort pursued in the sphere of social action consider the question of institutional capacity. After all, even the smallest group of individuals labouring at the grassroots must be able to maintain a consultative environment characterized by qualities of honesty, fairness, patience, tolerance, and courtesy. At a higher level of complexity, an organization dedicated to social action needs to develop the capacity to read society and identify the forces operating within it, to translate a vision of progress into projects and distinct, interconnected lines of action, to manage financial resources, and to interact with both governmental and non-governmental agencies.

The building of capacity in individuals and institutions goes hand in hand with the development of communities. In villages and neighbourhoods throughout the world, Bahá'ís are engaged in activities that enrich the devotional character of their communities, that tend to the spiritual education of children, that enhance the spiritual perception of junior youth and strengthen their powers of expression, and that enable increasing numbers to explore the application of the teachings of the Faith to their individual and collective lives. A process of community development, however, needs to reach beyond the level of activity and concern itself with those modes of expression and patterns of thought and behaviour that are to characterize a humanity which has come of age. In short, it must enter into the realm of culture. Viewed in this light, social action can become an occasion to raise collective consciousness of such vital principles as oneness, justice, and the equality of women and men; to promote an environment distinguished by traits such as truthfulness, equity, trustworthiness, and generosity; to enhance the ability of a community to resist the influence of destructive social forces; to demonstrate the value of cooperation as an organizing principle for activity; to fortify collective volition; and to infuse practice with insight from the teachings. For, in the final analysis, many of the questions most central to the emergence of a prosperous global civilization are to be addressed at the level of culture.

What seems necessary to acknowledge here is that the increase of capacity in each of these three protagonists does not occur in isolation; the development of any one is inextricably linked to the progress of the other two. The following statement of Shoghi Effendi speaks to this point:

"We cannot segregate the human heart from the environment outside us and say that once one of these is reformed everything will be improved. Man is organic with the world. His inner life moulds the environment and is itself also deeply affected by it. The one acts upon the other and every abiding change in the life of man is the result of these mutual reactions." (*Social Action*, A paper prepared by the Office of Social and Economic Development at the Bahá'í World Center, 26 November 2012)

Social action, it has been suggested in this paper, is to be carried out in the context of a much larger enterprise—namely, the advancement of a civilization that ensures the material and spiritual prosperity of the entire human race. The fundamental teachings of the Faith that will inspire this civilization, some of which have been mentioned in these pages, need to find expression in the sphere of social action. Clearly, the application of the requisite principles to the social and material progress of communities involves a vast process of learning.

In general, a challenge for any instance of social action is to ensure consistency—among the explicit and implicit convictions which underpin an initiative, the values promoted by it, the attitudes adopted by its participants, the methods they employ, and the ends they seek. Achieving consistency between belief and practice is no small task: a deep-seated recognition of the oneness of humanity should prevent all efforts from fostering disunity, isolation, separateness or competition; an unshakeable conviction in the nobility of human beings, capable of subduing their lower passions and evincing heavenly qualities, should serve to protect against prejudice and paternalism, both of which violate the dignity of people; an immutable belief in justice should guide an endeavour to allocate resources according to the real needs and aspirations of the community rather than the whims and wishes of a privileged few; the principle of the equality of women and men should open the way not only for women to assume their role as protagonists of development and benefit from its fruits but also for the experience of that half of the world's population to be given more and more emphasis in development thought. These few examples illustrate how closely spiritual principles are to guide development practice. (*Social Action*, A paper prepared by the Office of Social and Economic Development at the Bahá'í World Center, 26 November 2012)

The endeavours of the worldwide Bahá'í community can be seen in terms of a number of interacting processes—the spiritual enrichment of the individual, the development of local and national communities, the maturation of administrative institutions, to mention but a few—which trace their origins back to the time of Bahá'u'lláh Himself and which gathered strength during the ministries of 'Abdu'l-Bahá and Shoghi Effendi. Under the guidance of the Universal House of Justice, these processes have continued to advance steadily: the scope of their influence has gradually been extended and new dimensions added to their operation. Social and economic development is among them. This particular process, pursued most notably through a variety of educational activities down the years, received considerable impetus in 1983, when the House of Justice, in a message dated 20 October, asked for "systematic attention" to be given to this area of activity following the rapid expansion of the Bahá'í community during the 1970s.

The 1983 message emphasized that progress in the development field would depend largely on natural stirrings at the grassroots of the community. It also announced the establishment of the Office of Social and Economic Development (OSED) at the Bahá'í World Centre to "promote and coordinate the activities of the friends" in this field. Bahá'ís in every continent sought to respond to the call raised in the message in a number of ways, and the ensuing ten years constituted a period of experimentation, characterized simultaneously by enthusiasm and hesitation, thoughtful planning and haphazard action, achievements and setbacks. While most projects found it difficult to escape the patterns of development practice prevalent in the world, some offered glimpses of promising paradigms of action. From this initial decade of diverse activity, then, the Bahá'í community emerged with the pursuit of social and economic development firmly established as a feature of its organic life and with enhanced capacity to forge over time a distinctly Bahá'í approach.

In September 1993, the document "Bahá'í Social and Economic Development: Prospects for the Future," prepared at the World Centre, was approved by the Universal House of Justice for use by OSED in orienting and guiding the work in this area. It set the stage for the next ten years of activity and beyond. Drawing on the significant body of experience that had accumulated over the preceding decade, the document elaborated several features common to all such efforts. Awareness worldwide of the nature of Bahá'í social and economic development grew significantly during this period as a result, and a highly consistent, much more systematic approach began to take shape. The vision that emerged at the time called for the promotion of development activities at different levels of complexity. Most central to this vision was the question of capacity building. That activities should start on a modest scale and only grow in complexity in keeping with available human resources was a concept that gradually came to influence development thought and practice.

In 2001, the Universal House of Justice introduced to the Bahá'í world the concept of a cluster—a geographic construct, generally defined as a group of villages or as a city with its surrounding suburbs, intended to assist in planning and implementing activities associated with community life. This step was made possible by the establishment of training institutes at the national and regional levels during the 1990s, which employed a system of distance education to reach large numbers with a sequence of courses designed to increase capacity for service. The House of Justice encouraged the Bahá'í world to extend this system progressively to more and more clusters in order to promote their steady progress, laying first the strong spiritual foundations upon which a vibrant community life is built. Efforts in a cluster were initially to focus on the multiplication of certain core activities, open to all of the inhabitants, but with a view to developing the collective capacity needed to address in due time various aspects of the social and economic life of the population as well.

In the decade that followed, then, social action would increasingly come to be conceived within the context of the cluster. The conception of grass-roots social action that began to emerge was thus able to assume a much more pronounced collective dimension than had been previously articulated. During the same period, notable progress was also being made by OSED in its attempts to help systematize the experience of especially promising programmes and to learn about structures and methods required to enable communities around the world not only to benefit from them but to contribute to their further advancement. Today, in the establishment of continental and subcontinental offices—each serving either a network of sites for the dissemination of learning about the junior youth spiritual empowerment programme or a group of Bahá'í-inspired organizations dedicated to the promotion of some other educational programme—can be seen the first fruits of OSED's efforts to raise up structures across the globe to enhance collective capacity for this purpose. Underscoring the importance of what has been achieved so far, the Universal House of Justice wrote in its message dated 28 December 2010:

Eventually the strength of the institute process in the village, and the enhanced capabilities it has fostered in individuals, may enable the friends to take advantage of methods and programmes of proven effectiveness, which have been developed by one or another Bahá'í-inspired organization and which have been introduced into the cluster at the suggestion of, and with support from, our Office of Social and Economic Development.

Accomplishments over the past three decades in the area of social and economic development, then, combined with the consistent rise in human resources in clusters everywhere, have brought the Bahá'í world to a new stage in its efforts to engage in grassroots social action. (*Social Action*, A paper prepared by the Office of Social and Economic Development at the Bahá'í World Center, 26 November 2012)

Universal Participation in Social Action

A civilization befitting a humanity which, having passed through earlier stages of social evolution, is coming of age will not emerge through the efforts exerted by a select group of nations or even a network of national and international agencies. Rather, the challenge must be faced by all of humanity. Every member of the human family has not only the right to benefit from a materially and spiritually prosperous civilization but also an obligation to contribute towards its construction. Social action should operate, then, on the principle of universal participation.

Issues related to participation have been discussed at length in development literature. Yet, in both theory and practice, this vital principle has often been approached at the level of technique—for example, through the utilization of surveys and focus groups. Such tools, of course, have their merits, as do more ambitious efforts intended to increase participation in political processes or to offer training to the beneficiaries of services delivered by one or another governmental or non-governmental agency. Still, these measures seem to fall short of the kind of participation envisioned above. What appears to be called for in any given region, microregion or cluster is the involvement of a growing number of people in a collective process of learning, one which is focused on the nature and dynamics of a path that conduces to the material and spiritual progress of their villages or neighbourhoods. Such a process would allow its participants to engage in the generation, application, and diffusion of knowledge, a most potent and indispensable force in the advancement of civilization.

In this connection, it is important to realize that the application and propagation of existing knowledge is invariably accompanied by the generation of new knowledge—much of which takes the form of insights acquired through experience. Here the systematization of learning is crucial. As a group of people working at the grassroots begins to gain experience in social action, the first lessons learned may consist of little more than occasional stories, anecdotes, and personal accounts. Over time, patterns tend to emerge which can be documented and carefully analysed. To facilitate the systematization of knowledge, appropriate structures have to be put in place at the local level, among them institutions and agencies invested with authority to safeguard the integrity of the learning process and to ensure that it is not reduced to opinion or the mere collection of various experiences—in short, to see to it that veritable knowledge is generated. In this regard, the authority invested in the institutions of the Administrative Order working at the grassroots to harmonize individual volition with collective will endows the Bahá'í community with a remarkable capacity to nurture participation.

No matter how essential, a process of learning at the local level will remain limited in its effectiveness if it is not connected to a global process concerned with the material and spiritual prosperity of humanity as a whole. Structures are required, then, at all levels, from the local to the international, to facilitate learning about development. At the international level, such learning calls for a degree of conceptualization that takes into account the broader processes of global transformation under way and which serves to adjust the overall direction of development activities accordingly. In this respect, OSED sees itself as a learning entity dedicated to the systematization of a growing worldwide experience made possible by the participation of increasing numbers of individuals, agencies, and communities. As this participation widens, the Office strives to develop its own capacity to observe activity at the grassroots, to identify and analyse patterns that emerge under one or more sets of circumstances, and to disseminate the knowledge thus generated, strengthening structures for this purpose and lending impetus to the process of learning at all levels. The approach to development that comes into focus, then, defies categorization into either "top-down" or "bottom-up"; it is one, rather, of reciprocity and interconnectedness. (*Social Action*, A paper prepared by the Office of Social and Economic Development at the Bahá'í World Center, 26 November 2012)

The methodology of Bahá'í Social and Economic Development

In addition to those elements of the conceptual framework that define the nature of Bahá'í development efforts, there are a number of concepts which shed light on the methods to be adopted. That the collective investigation of reality can best be undertaken in an atmosphere which encourages detachment from personal views, that such an ongoing investigation should give due importance to valid empirical information, that mere opinion should not be raised to the status of fact, that conclusions should correspond to the complexity of the issues at hand and not be broken up into a series of simplistic points, that the articulation of observations and conclusions should be presented in precise and dispassionate language, that progress in every area of endeavour is contingent upon the creation of an environment where powers are multiplied and manifest themselves in unified action—general concepts such as these, drawn from both science and religion, inform the specific methodological perspective discussed below.

READING SOCIETY AND FORMULATING A VISION

As mentioned earlier, endeavours in the sphere of social action frequently take the form of modest acts carried out by small groups of individuals residing in a locality. In a sense, these stirrings at the grassroots can be considered responses to readings of social reality, even though they are seldom expressed explicitly as such at that level. For more elaborate endeavours of social and economic development, reading society with higher and higher degrees of accuracy has to become an explicit element of the methodology of learning.

Every development effort can be said to represent a response to some understanding of the nature and state of society, its challenges, the institutions operating in it, the forces influencing it, and the capacities of its peoples. To read society in this way is not to explore every detail of the social reality. Nor does it necessarily involve formal studies. Conditions need to be understood progressively, both from the perspective of a particular endeavour's purpose and in the context of a vision of humanity's collective existence. Indeed, it is vital that the reading of society be consistent with the teachings of the Faith. That the true nature of a human being is spiritual, that every human being is a "mine rich in gems" of limitless potential, that the forces of integration and disintegration each in their own way are propelling humanity towards its destiny are but a few examples of teachings that would shape one's understanding of social reality. Bahá'í-inspired organizations supporting relatively complex lines of action need to continually refine their reading of society, using the methods of science to the best of their abilities.

It is important to note that reading the social reality of a population from within is different than studying it as an outsider. In instances where the population in question is relatively poor in material resources, outsiders with access to greater means frequently see only deprivation—the wealth of talent in the population, the aspirations of its members, and their capacity to arise and become the protagonists of change may all be overlooked. Furthermore, external observers of poverty are all too often unaware of the tendency to allow their own feelings of pity, fear, indignation or ambivalence to affect their reading of society and to base their proposed solutions on the value they place on their own experiences. However, when an effort is participatory, in the sense that it seeks to involve the people themselves in the generation and application of knowledge, as all forge together a path of progress, dualities such as "outsider-insider" and "knowledgeable-ignorant" quickly disappear.

According to their reading of society, those engaged in social action form and refine a vision of their work within the social space available to them. The word "vision" here does not simply mean a set of goals or a description of an idealized future condition. Particularly when a Bahá'í-inspired organization is involved, a vision has to express a general idea of how goals are to be achieved: the nature of the strategies to be devised, the approaches to be taken, the attitudes to be assumed, and even an outline of some of the methods to be employed. The vision of work articulated by such an organization is never complete; it has to become more and more precise, be able to accommodate constantly evolving and ever more complex action, and attain increasingly high levels of accuracy in its operation.

CONSULTATION

If learning in action is to be the primary mode of operation in the area of social and economic development, the Bahá'í principle of consultation needs

to be fully appreciated. Whether concerned with analysing a specific problem, attaining higher degrees of understanding on a given issue, or exploring
possible courses of action, consultation may be seen as collective search for
truth. Participants in a consultative process see reality from different points
of view, and as these views are examined and understood, clarity is achieved.
In this conception of the collective investigation of reality, truth is not a
compromise between opposing interest groups. Nor does the desire to exercise power over one another animate participants in the consultative process.
What they seek, rather, is the power of unified thought and action.

In the context of social action, the principle of consultation is expressed
in a variety of forms, each appropriate to the space within which it occurs.
Often, when a small group is engaged in an endeavour, every matter of
concern is the subject of consultation. Yet, within an organization, the
principle will find expression in different ways. What should be noted in
this connection is that, at times, consultation is undertaken between those
regarded as equals with the aim of reaching a joint decision, as in the case
of the deliberations of a Spiritual Assembly. Under other circumstances, it
takes the form of a discussion, as may be necessary, to draw out thoughts and
information towards the enrichment of common understanding, but with
the decision being made by those with authority. It is this latter form that
would distinguish the operations of a Bahá'í-inspired organization, where a
degree of individual or group authority is given to those on whom responsibility has been conferred.

Clearly, then, not every person within an organization will participate
equally in making every decision. Responsibility needs to be appropriately
structured and defined. For example, there will be many spaces in which
individuals involved in a particular component of the work will have the
opportunity to share insights, reach higher levels of understanding, and
make certain decisions pertaining to their area of functioning. In the case of
an organization with a board and an executive director, they will often take
decisions without the need to consult with every member of the organization. But theirs is also the responsibility to create an atmosphere in which

relevant information and knowledge flow openly and in which the results of consultation in all the spaces of the organization are conveyed in ways that promote understanding and consensus among its members.

Beyond such considerations, a consultative spirit pervades the interactions of those engaged in social action, of whatever size and complexity, and the population they serve. This does not imply that formal mechanisms are necessarily in place for this purpose. It suggests, rather, that the aspirations of the people, their observations and ideas, are ever present and are consciously incorporated into plans and programmes.

ACTION AND REFLECTION ON ACTION

At the heart of every development endeavour is consistent, systematic action. Action, however, needs to be accompanied by constant reflection to ensure that it continues to serve the aims of the endeavour. Development strategies that are formulated simply in terms of projects with well-stated goals, followed by evaluation of how and why they were or were not achieved, have limitations. An approach to development defined in terms of learning does, at times, admit formal evaluation. Yet, it depends far more on structured reflection woven into a pattern of action, through which questions can emerge and methods and approaches be adjusted.

Given the multitude of humanity's needs and the enthusiasm with which programmes inspired by the teachings of the Faith are frequently received, it can be tempting for a Bahá'í-inspired organization to try to pursue every opportunity and become engaged in frenetic action. Learning to be systematic and focused is a challenge that all those involved in development efforts, from a small group to the community itself, have to meet.

A notion that has proven useful in this respect is that of a line of action. A line of action is conceived as a sequence of activities, each of which builds on the previous one and prepares the way for the next. Endeavours often begin with a single line of action, but gradually a number of interrelated lines emerge, constituting a whole area of action. For example, to be effective, even an effort at the grassroots focusing solely on the area of child education needs to simultaneously follow such lines of action as the training of teachers and consciousness-raising in the community about education, as well as attending to the teaching-learning experience.

Focused, systematic thinking and persistent, meticulous labour do not, of course, detract from the spirit of service that animates social action. While paying attention to the smallest practical details, one can be occupied with the most profound spiritual matters. A distinguishing feature of any Bahá'í endeavour has to be the emphasis it places on the spirit with which action is undertaken. This requires from the participants purity of motive, rectitude of conduct, humility, selflessness, and respect for human dignity. As Bahá'u'lláh states:

One righteous act is endowed with a potency that can so elevate the dust as to cause it to pass beyond the heaven of heavens. It can tear every bond asunder, and hath the power to restore the force that hath spent itself and vanished.

Utilizing material means

To accomplish their aims, endeavours in the area of social action require material means. There is a tendency among many organizations in the world—including those working to achieve praiseworthy ends—to measure success principally in terms of the amount of money received and spent. Bahá'í development efforts are expected to set aside such criteria. In modest instances of social action, resources are typically contributed by the community. A more complex endeavour will have to acquire greater capacity to draw upon and utilize funds. In the case of a Bahá'í-inspired organization, this may extend, as mentioned earlier, to receiving grants from donor agencies. Here great care is required to ensure that, in attempting to secure funds, an organization is not distracted from its primary purpose: capacity building within a given population.

However modest the amounts expended may be, it is vital that a system be put in place to oversee the proper management of finances. The integrity of an endeavour is, of course, secured by the trustworthiness and honesty of its participants. Yet, a proven system of financial management within an organization serves to protect against an atmosphere of carelessness and imprecision that can open the door to temptation.

In addition to a sound financial system, the question of efficiency needs attention. What should be avoided are limited conceptions of efficiency, for instance, those that consider only the relation of output to material input, even when the latter includes some quantitative measure of effort. A more sophisticated understanding of efficiency seems to be required. With regard to input, for example, work that is motivated by a spirit of service and an inner urge to excel clearly has a different value than work that is used as a vehicle to advance one's personal interests. As to results, to give another example, the accomplishment of a particular task—say, the construction of a small facility for a school—may be far less important than the development of the participants' capacity to cooperate and engage in unified action.

There is also a wealth of spiritual and intellectual resources upon which endeavours can draw, whatever the material resources available. A number of these are mentioned in the Bahá'í writings, such as "unrelaxing resolve and harmonious cooperation," "energy, loyalty and resourcefulness," "determination," "spirit of absolute consecration," "organizing ability," "zeal," "tenacity, sagacity and fidelity," "single-minded devotion," "absolute dedication," "perseverance," "vigour," "courage," "audacity," "consistency," "tenacity of purpose," "tenacity of resolution," and "unrelaxing vigilance." What the Bahá'í community has so far achieved in the work of expansion and consolidation with limited material means is a testimony to the efficacy of these spiritual resources, which should be increasingly extended to the sphere of social action.

Those involved in social action also need to be constantly aware of the solemn responsibility for the money that has been placed at their disposal. In this connection, it is helpful to keep in mind the attitude Bahá'ís evince in relation to the sacred funds of the Faith—contributions are offered liberally, joyfully, and sacrificially, and institutions observe prudence and a high degree of economy in the expenditure of that money. (*Social Action*, A paper prepared by the Office of Social and Economic Development at the Bahá'í World Center, 26 November 2012)

9

RELIGION'S VITAL ROLE IN HUMAN PROGRESS

The purpose of religion as revealed from the heaven of God's holy Will is to establish unity and concord amongst the peoples of the world; make it not the cause of dissension and strife. The religion of God and His divine law are the most potent instruments and the surest of all means for the dawning of the light of unity amongst men. The progress of the world, the development of nations, the tranquility of peoples, and the peace of all who dwell on earth are among the principles and ordinances of God. Religion bestoweth upon man the most precious of all gifts, offereth the cup of prosperity, imparteth eternal life, and showereth imperishable benefits upon mankind.

—Bahá'u'lláh, *Tablets of Bahá'u'lláh*, pp. 129–30

The Goal of Religion

O ye that dwell on earth! The religion of God is for love and unity; make it not the cause of enmity or dissension. In the eyes of men of insight and the beholders of the Most Sublime Vision, whatsoever are the effective means for safeguarding and promoting the happiness and welfare of the children of men have already been revealed by the Pen of Glory. (Bahá'u'lláh, *Tablets of Bahá'u'lláh*, p. 220)

The fundamental purpose animating the Faith of God and His Religion is to safeguard the interests and promote the unity of the human race, and to foster the spirit of love and fellowship amongst men. Suffer it not to become a source of dissension and discord, of hate and enmity. This is the straight Path, the fixed and immovable foundation. Whatsoever is raised on this foundation, the changes and chances of the world can never impair its strength, nor will the revolution of countless centuries undermine its structure. (Bahá'u'lláh, *Gleanings from the Writings of Bahá'u'lláh*, no. 110.1)

Regard the world as the human body which, though at its creation whole and perfect, hath been afflicted, through various causes, with grave disorders and maladies. Not for one day did it gain ease, nay its sickness waxed more severe, as it fell under the treatment of ignorant physicians, who gave full rein to their personal desires, and have erred grievously. And if, at one time, through the care of an able physician, a member of that body was healed, the rest remained afflicted as before. Thus informeth you the All-Knowing, the All-Wise. (Bahá'u'lláh, *Epistle to the Son of the Wolf*, p. 62)

The body politic today is greatly in need of a physician. It is similar to a human body afflicted with severe ailments. A doctor diagnoses the case and prescribes treatment. He does not prescribe, however, until he has made the diagnosis. The disease which afflicts the body politic is lack of love and absence of altruism. In the hearts of men no real love is found, and the condition is such that, unless their susceptibilities are quickened by some power so that unity, love and accord may develop within them, there can be no healing, no agreement among mankind. Love and unity are the needs of the body politic today. Without these there can be no progress or prosperity attained. ('Abdu'l-Bahá, *The Promulgation of Universal Peace*, p. 237)

The essential purpose of the religion of God is to establish unity among mankind. The divine Manifestations were Founders of the means of fellowship and love. They did not come to create discord, strife and hatred in the world. The religion of God is the cause of love, but if it is made to be the source of enmity and bloodshed, surely its absence is preferable to its existence; for then it becomes satanic, detrimental and an obstacle to the human world. ('Abdu'l-Bahá, *The Promulgation of Universal Peace*, p. 282)

"There are," 'Abdu'l-Bahá remarked, "some who imagine that an innate sense of human dignity will prevent man from committing evil actions and ensure his spiritual and material perfection." On the contrary, He pointed out, it is readily observable that human development depends on education. He then drew the implications of this law for the progress of society. All the evidence inescapably demonstrates that the principal influence in the gradual civilizing of human character, far from being a simple endowment of nature, has been the effect produced on the rational soul by the guidance of the successive Messengers of God. It has been through Their intervention, and through it alone, that the peoples of the world, of whatever nation or religion, have learned the values and ideals that have empowered them to put material resources and technological means at the service of human betterment. It is They who, in each age, have defined the meaning and requirements of modernity. It is They who have been the ultimate Educators of humankind:

Universal benefits derive from the grace of the Divine religions, for they lead their true followers to sincerity of intent, to high purpose, to purity and spotless honour, to surpassing kindness and compassion, to the keeping of their covenants when they have covenanted, to concern for the rights of others, to liberality, to justice in every aspect of life, to humanity and philanthropy, to valour and to unflagging efforts in the service of mankind. It is religion, to sum up, which produces all human virtues, and it is these virtues which are the bright candles of civilization. (The Universal House of Justice, letter dated 26 November 2003, to the Followers of Bahá'u'lláh in the Cradle of the Faith)

So far as earthly existence is concerned, many of the greatest achievements of religion have been moral in character. Through its teachings and through the examples of human lives illumined by these teachings, masses of people in all ages and lands have developed the capacity to love. They have learned to discipline the animal side of their natures, to make great sacrifices for the common good, to practice forgiveness, generosity, and trust, to use wealth and other resources in ways that serve the advancement of civilization. Institutional systems have been devised to translate these moral advances into the norms of social life on a vast scale. However obscured by dogmatic accretions and diverted by sectarian conflict, the spiritual impulses set in motion by such transcendent figures as Krishna, Moses, Buddha, Zoroaster, Jesus, and Muhammad have been the chief influence in the civilizing of human character. (Bahá'í International Community, *The Prosperity of Humankind*)

The Prophets of God Were United in Purpose

The strife between religions, nations and races arises from misunderstanding. If we investigate the religions to discover the principles underlying their foundations, we will find they agree; for the fundamental reality of them is one and not multiple. By this means the religionists of the world will reach their point of unity and reconciliation. They will ascertain the truth that the purpose of religion is the acquisition of praiseworthy virtues, the betterment of morals, the spiritual development of mankind, the real life and divine bestowals. All the Prophets have been the promoters of these principles; none of Them has been the promoter of corruption, vice or evil. They have summoned mankind to all good. They have united people in the love of God, invited them to the religions of the unity of mankind and exhorted them to amity and agreement. ('Abdu'l-Bahá, *The Promulgation of Universal Peace,* p. 210)

The central purpose of the divine religions is the establishment of peace and unity among mankind. Their reality is one; therefore, their accomplishment is one and universal—whether it be through the essential or material ordinances of God. There is but one light of the material sun, one ocean, one rain, one atmosphere. Similarly, in the spiritual world there is one divine reality forming the center and altruistic basis for peace and reconciliation among various and conflicting nations and peoples. ('Abdu'l-Bahá, *The Promulgation of Universal Peace*, pp. 135–36)

The purpose of all the divine religions is the establishment of the bonds of love and fellowship among men, and the heavenly phenomena of the revealed Word of God are intended to be a source of knowledge and illumination to humanity. So long as man persists in his adherence to ancestral forms and imitation of obsolete ceremonials, denying higher revelations of the divine light in the world, strife and contention will destroy the purpose of religion and make love and fellowship impossible. Each of the holy Manifestations announced the glad tidings of His successor, and each One confirmed the message of His predecessor. Therefore, inasmuch as They were agreed and united in purpose and teaching, it is incumbent upon Their followers to be likewise unified in love and spiritual fellowship. In no other way will discord and alienation disappear and the oneness of the world of humanity be established. ('Abdu'l-Bahá, *The Promulgation of Universal Peace*, p. 481)

When reality envelops the soul of man, love is possible. The divine purpose in religion is pure love and agreement. The Prophets of God manifested complete love for all. Each One announced the glad tidings of His successor, and each subsequent One confirmed the teachings and prophecies of the Prophet Who preceded Him. There was no disagreement or variance in the reality of Their teaching and mission. Discord has arisen among Their followers, who have lost sight of reality and hold fast to imitations. If imitations be done away with and the radiant shining reality dawn in the souls of men, love and unity must prevail. In this way humanity will be rescued from the strife and wars which have prevailed for thousands of years; dissensions will pass away and the illumination of unity dawn. Consider how all the Prophets of God were persecuted and what hardships They experienced. Jesus Christ endured affliction and accepted martyrdom upon the cross in order to summon mankind to unity and love. What sacrifice could be greater? He brought the religion of love and fellowship into the world. Shall we make use of it to create discord, violence and hatred among mankind?

Moses was persecuted and driven out into the desert, Abraham was banished, Muhammad took refuge in caves, the Báb was killed and Bahá'u'lláh was exiled and imprisoned forty years. Yet all of Them desired fellowship and love among men. They endured hardships, suffered persecution and death for our sakes that we might be taught to love one another and be united and affiliated instead of discordant and at variance. Enough of these long centuries which have brought such vicissitudes and hardships into the world through strife and hatred. Now in this radiant century let us try to do the will of God that we may be rescued from these things of darkness and come forth into the boundless illumination of heaven, shunning division and welcoming the divine oneness of humanity. Perchance, God willing, this terrestrial world may become as a celestial mirror upon which we may behold the imprint of the traces of Divinity, and the fundamental qualities of a new creation may be reflected from the reality of love shining in human hearts. From the light and semblance of God in us may it be, indeed, proved and witnessed that God has created man after His own image and likeness. ('Abdu'l-Bahá, *The Promulgation of Universal Peace*, pp. 327–28)

The endowments which distinguish the human race from all other forms of life are summed up in what is known as the human spirit; the mind is its essential quality. These endowments have enabled humanity to build civilizations and to prosper materially. But such accomplishments alone have never satisfied the human spirit, whose mysterious nature inclines it towards transcendence, a reaching towards an invisible realm, towards the ultimate reality, that unknowable essence of essences called God. The religions brought to mankind by a succession of spiritual luminaries have been the primary link between humanity and that ultimate reality, and have galvanized and refined mankind's capacity to achieve spiritual success together with social progress.

No serious attempt to set human affairs aright, to achieve world peace, can ignore religion. Man's perception and practice of it are largely the stuff of history. An eminent historian described religion as a "faculty of human nature." That the perversion of this faculty has contributed to much of the confusion in society and the conflicts in and between individuals can hardly be denied. But neither can any fair-minded observer discount the preponderating influence exerted by religion on the vital expressions of civilization. Furthermore, its indispensability to social order has repeatedly been demonstrated by its direct effect on laws and morality.

Writing of religion as a social force, Bahá'u'lláh said: "Religion is the greatest of all means for the establishment of order in the world and for the peaceful contentment of all that dwell therein." Referring to the eclipse or corruption of religion, he wrote: "Should the lamp of religion be obscured, chaos and confusion will ensue, and the lights of fairness, of justice, of tranquility and peace cease to shine." In an enumeration of such consequences the Bahá'í writings point out that the "perversion of human nature, the degradation of human conduct, the corruption and dissolution of human institutions, reveal themselves, under such circumstances, in their worst and most revolting aspects. Human character is debased, confidence is shaken, the nerves of discipline are relaxed, the voice of human conscience is stilled, the sense of decency and shame is obscured, conceptions of duty, of solidarity, of reciprocity and loyalty are distorted, and the very feeling of peacefulness, of joy and of hope is gradually extinguished."

If, therefore, humanity has come to a point of paralyzing conflict it must look to itself, to its own negligence, to the siren voices to which it has listened, for the source of the misunderstandings and confusion perpetrated in the name of religion. Those who have held blindly and selfishly to their particular orthodoxies, who have imposed on their votaries erroneous and conflicting interpretations of the pronouncements of the Prophets of God, bear heavy responsibility for this confusion—a confusion compounded by the artificial barriers erected between faith and reason, science and religion. For from a fair-minded examination of the actual utterances of the Founders of the great religions, and of the social milieus in which they were obliged to carry out their missions, there is nothing to support the contentions and prejudices deranging the religious communities of mankind and therefore all human affairs.

The teaching that we should treat others as we ourselves would wish to be treated, an ethic variously repeated in all the great religions, lends force to this latter observation in two particular respects: it sums up the moral attitude, the peace-inducing aspect, extending through these religions irrespective of their place or time of origin; it also signifies an aspect of unity which is their essential virtue, a virtue mankind in its disjointed view of history has failed to appreciate.

Had humanity seen the Educators of its collective childhood in their true character, as agents of one civilizing process, it would no doubt have reaped incalculably greater benefits from the cumulative effects of their successive missions. This, alas, it failed to do.

The resurgence of fanatical religious fervour occurring in many lands cannot be regarded as more than a dying convulsion. The very nature of the violent and disruptive phenomena associated with it testifies to the spiritual bankruptcy it represents. Indeed, one of the strangest and saddest features of the current outbreak of religious fanaticism is the extent to which, in each case, it is undermining not only the spiritual values which are conducive to the unity of mankind but also those unique moral victories won by the particular religion it purports to serve.

However vital a force religion has been in the history of mankind, and however dramatic the current resurgence of militant religious fanaticism, religion and religious institutions have, for many decades, been viewed by increasing numbers of people as irrelevant to the major concerns of the modern world. In its place they have turned either to the hedonistic pursuit of material satisfactions or to the following of man-made ideologies designed to rescue society from the evident evils under which it groans. All too many of these ideologies, alas, instead of embracing the concept of the oneness of mankind and promoting the increase of concord among different peoples, have tended to deify the state, to subordinate the rest of mankind to one nation, race or class, to attempt to suppress all discussion and interchange of ideas, or to callously abandon starving millions to the operations of a market system that all too clearly is aggravating the plight of the majority of mankind, while enabling small sections to live in a condition of affluence scarcely dreamed of by our forebears.

How tragic is the record of the substitute faiths that the worldly-wise of our age have created. In the massive disillusionment of entire populations who have been taught to worship at their altars can be read history's irreversible verdict on their value. The fruits these doctrines have produced, after decades of an increasingly unrestrained exercise of power by those who owe their ascendancy in human affairs to them, are the social and economic ills that blight every region of our world in the closing years of the twentieth century. Underlying all these outward afflictions is the spiritual damage reflected in the apathy that has gripped the mass of the peoples of all nations and by the extinction of hope in the hearts of deprived and anguished millions. (The Universal House of Justice, *The Promise of World Peace*, ¶12–20)

A Progressive Revelation of Divine Guidance
The All-Knowing Physician hath His finger on the pulse of mankind. He perceiveth the disease, and prescribeth, in His unerring wisdom, the remedy. Every age hath its own problem, and every soul its particular aspiration. The remedy the world needeth in its present-day afflictions can never be the same as that which a subsequent age may require. Be anxiously concerned with the needs of the age ye live in, and center your deliberations on its exigencies and requirements. (Bahá'u'lláh, *Gleanings from the Writings of Bahá'u'lláh*, no. 106.1)

And now concerning thy question regarding the nature of religion. Know thou that they who are truly wise have likened the world unto the human temple. As the body of man needeth a garment to clothe it, so the body of mankind must needs be adorned with the mantle of justice and wisdom.

195

Its robe is the Revelation vouchsafed unto it by God. Whenever this robe hath fulfilled its purpose, the Almighty will assuredly renew it. For every age requireth a fresh measure of the light of God. Every Divine Revelation hath been sent down in a manner that befitted the circumstances of the age in which it hath appeared. (Bahá'u'lláh, *Gleanings from the Writings of Bahá'u'lláh*, no. 34.7)

The greatest bestowal of God to man is the capacity to attain human virtues. Therefore, the teachings of religion must be reformed and renewed because past teachings are not suitable for the present time. For example, the sciences of bygone centuries are not adequate for the present because sciences have undergone reform. The industrialism of the past will not ensure present efficiency because industrialism has advanced. The laws of the past are being superseded because they are not applicable to this time. All material conditions pertaining to the world of humanity have undergone reform, have achieved development, and the institutes of the past are not to be compared with those of this age. The laws and institutes of former governments cannot be current today, for legislation must be in conformity with the needs and requirements of the body politic at this time.

This has been the case also with the religious teachings so long set forth in the temples and churches, because they were not based upon the fundamental principles of the religions of God. In other words, the foundation of the divine religions had become obscured and nonessentials of form and ceremony were adhered to—that is, the kernel of religion had apparently disappeared, and only the shell remained. Consequently, it was necessary that the fundamental basis of all religious teaching should be restored, that the Sun of Reality which had set should rise again, that the springtime which had refreshed the arena of life in ages gone by should appear anew, that the rain which had ceased should descend, that the breezes which had become stilled should blow once more. ('Abdu'l-Bahá, *The Promulgation of Universal Peace*, pp. 534–35)

Today the world of humanity is walking in darkness because it is out of touch with the world of God. That is why we do not see the signs of God in the hearts of men. The power of the Holy Spirit has no influence. When a divine spiritual illumination becomes manifest in the world of humanity, when divine instruction and guidance appear, then enlightenment follows, a new spirit is realized within, a new power descends, and a new life is given. It is like the birth from the animal kingdom into the kingdom of man. When man acquires these virtues, the oneness of the world of humanity will be revealed, the banner of international peace will be upraised, equality between all mankind will be realized, and the Orient and Occident will become one. Then will the justice of God become manifest, all humanity will appear as the members of one family, and every member of that family will be consecrated to cooperation and mutual assistance. ('Abdu'l-Bahá, *The Promulgation of Universal Peace,* pp. 424–25)

The fundamental principle enunciated by Bahá'u'lláh . . . is that religious truth is not absolute but relative, that Divine Revelation is a continuous and progressive process, that all the great religions of the world are divine in origin, that their basic principles are in complete harmony, that their aims and purposes are one and the same, that their teachings are but facets of one truth, that their functions are complementary, that they differ only in the nonessential aspects of their doctrines, and that their missions represent successive stages in the spiritual evolution of human society. . . .

. . . His mission is to proclaim that the ages of the infancy and of the childhood of the human race are past, that the convulsions associated with the present stage of its adolescence are slowly and painfully preparing it to attain the stage of manhood, and are heralding the approach of that Age of Ages when swords will be beaten into plowshares, when the Kingdom promised by Jesus Christ will have been established, and the peace of the planet definitely and permanently ensured. Nor does Bahá'u'lláh claim finality for His own Revelation, but rather stipulates that a fuller measure of the truth

He has been commissioned by the Almighty to vouchsafe to humanity, at so critical a juncture in its fortunes, must needs be disclosed at future stages in the constant and limitless evolution of mankind. (Shoghi Effendi, Statement to the UN Committee on Palestine, 1947)

"It hath been decreed by Us," explains Bahá'u'lláh, "that the Word of God, and all the potentialities thereof, shall be manifested unto men in strict conformity with such conditions as have been foreordained by Him Who is the All-Knowing, the All-Wise. . . . Should the Word be allowed to release suddenly all the energies latent within it, no man could sustain the weight of so mighty a Revelation." "All created things," 'Abdu'l-Bahá, elucidating this truth, has affirmed, "have their degree or stage of maturity. The period of maturity in the life of a tree is the time of its fruit-bearing. . . . The animal attains a stage of full growth and completeness, and in the human kingdom man reaches his maturity when the light of his intelligence attains its greatest power and development. . . . Similarly there are periods and stages in the collective life of humanity. At one time it was passing through its stage of childhood, at another its period of youth, but now it has entered its long-predicted phase of maturity, the evidences of which are everywhere apparent. . . . That which was applicable to human needs during the early history of the race can neither meet nor satisfy the demands of this day, this period of newness and consummation. Humanity has emerged from its former state of limitation and preliminary training. Man must now become imbued with new virtues and powers, new moral standards, new capacities. New bounties, perfect bestowals, are awaiting and already descending upon him. The gifts and blessings of the period of youth, although timely and sufficient during the adolescence of mankind, are now incapable of meeting the requirements of its maturity." "In every Dispensation," He moreover has written, "the light of Divine Guidance has been focused upon one central theme. . . . In this wondrous Revelation, this glorious century, the foundation of the Faith of God, and the distinguishing feature of His Law, is the consciousness of the oneness of mankind." (Shoghi Effendi, *The Promised Day is Come,* ¶292)

The Promise of the Future

God's purpose is none other than to usher in, in ways He alone can bring about, and the full significance of which He alone can fathom, the Great, the Golden Age of a long-divided, a long-afflicted humanity. Its present state, indeed even its immediate future, is dark, distressingly dark. Its distant future, however, is radiant, gloriously radiant—so radiant that no eye can visualize it.

"The winds of despair," writes Bahá'u'lláh, as He surveys the immediate destinies of mankind, "are, alas, blowing from every direction, and the strife that divides and afflicts the human race is daily increasing. The signs of impending convulsions and chaos can now be discerned, inasmuch as the prevailing order appears to be lamentably defective." "Such shall be its plight," He, in another connection, has declared, "that to disclose it now would not be meet and seemly." "These fruitless strifes," He, on the other hand, contemplating the future of mankind, has emphatically prophesied, in the course of His memorable interview with the Persian orientalist, Edward G. Browne, "these ruinous wars shall pass away, and the 'Most Great Peace' shall come. . . . These strifes and this bloodshed and discord must cease, and all men be as one kindred and one family." "Soon," He predicts, "will the present-day order be rolled up, and a new one spread out in its stead." "After a time," He also has written, "all the governments on earth will change. Oppression will envelop the world. And following a universal convulsion, the sun of justice will rise from the horizon of the unseen realm." "The whole earth," He, moreover, has stated, "is now in a state of pregnancy. The day is approaching when it will have yielded its noblest fruits, when from it will have sprung forth the loftiest trees, the most enchanting blossoms, the most heavenly blessings." "All nations and kindreds," 'Abdu'l-Bahá likewise has written, ". . . will become a single nation. Religious and sectarian antagonism, the hostility of races and peoples, and differences among nations, will be eliminated. All men will adhere to one religion, will have one common faith, will be blended into one race, and become a single people. All will dwell in one common fatherland, which is the planet itself." (Shoghi Effendi, *The Promised Day is Come,* ¶287)

The long ages of infancy and childhood, through which the human race had to pass, have receded into the background. Humanity is now experiencing the commotions invariably associated with the most turbulent stage of its evolution, the stage of adolescence, when the impetuosity of youth and its vehemence reach their climax, and must gradually be superseded by the calmness, the wisdom, and the maturity that characterize the stage of manhood. Then will the human race reach that stature of ripeness which will enable it to acquire all the powers and capacities upon which its ultimate development must depend.

Unification of the whole of mankind is the hall-mark of the stage which human society is now approaching. Unity of family, of tribe, of city-state, and nation have been successively attempted and fully established. World unity is the goal towards which a harassed humanity is striving. Nation-building has come to an end. The anarchy inherent in state sovereignty is moving towards a climax. A world, growing to maturity, must abandon this fetish, recognize the oneness and wholeness of human relationships, and establish once for all the machinery that can best incarnate this fundamental principle of its life.

"A new life," Bahá'u'lláh proclaims, "is, in this age, stirring within all the peoples of the earth; and yet none hath discovered its cause, or perceived its motive." "O ye children of men," He thus addresses His generation, "the fundamental purpose animating the Faith of God and His Religion is to safeguard the interests and promote the unity of the human race. . . . This is the straight path, the fixed and immovable foundation. Whatsoever is raised on this foundation, the changes and chances of the world can never impair its strength, nor will the revolution of countless centuries undermine its structure." "The well-being of mankind," He declares, "its peace and security are unattainable unless and until its unity is firmly established." "So powerful is the light of unity," is His further testimony, "that it can illuminate the whole earth. The one true God, He Who knoweth all things, Himself testifieth to the truth of these words. . . . This goal excelleth every other goal, and this aspiration is the monarch of all aspirations." "He Who is your Lord, the All-Merciful," He, moreover, has written, "cherisheth in His heart the desire of beholding the entire human race as one soul and one body. Haste ye to win your share of God's good grace and mercy in this Day that eclipseth all other created days." (Shoghi Effendi, *The World Order of Bahá'u'lláh*, pp. 202–3)

. . . Bahá'u'lláh, we should readily recognize, has not only imbued mankind with a new and regenerating Spirit. He has not merely enunciated certain universal principles, or propounded a particular philosophy, however potent, sound and universal these may be. In addition to these He, as well as 'Abdu'l-Bahá after Him, has, unlike the Dispensations of the past, clearly and specifically laid down a set of Laws, established definite institutions, and provided for the essentials of a Divine Economy. These are destined to be a pattern for future society, a supreme instrument for the establishment of the Most Great Peace, and the one agency for the unification of the world, and the proclamation of the reign of righteousness and justice upon the earth. (Shoghi Effendi, *The World Order of Bahá'u'lláh*, p. 19)

The Great Peace towards which people of goodwill throughout the centuries have inclined their hearts, of which seers and poets for countless generations have expressed their vision, and for which from age to age the sacred scriptures of mankind have constantly held the promise, is now at long last within the reach of the nations. For the first time in history it is possible for everyone to view the entire planet, with all its myriad diversified peoples, in one perspective. World peace is not only possible but inevitable. It is the next stage in the evolution of this planet—in the words of one great thinker, "the planetization of mankind."

RELIGION'S VITAL ROLE
IN HUMAN PROGRESS

Whether peace is to be reached only after unimaginable horrors precipitated by humanity's stubborn clinging to old patterns of behavior, or is to be embraced now by an act of consultative will, is the choice before all who inhabit the earth. At this critical juncture when the intractable problems confronting nations have been fused into one common concern for the whole world, failure to stem the tide of conflict and disorder would be unconscionably irresponsible. (The Universal House of Justice, *The Promise of World Peace*, ¶1–2)

In contemplating the supreme importance of the task now challenging the entire world, we bow our heads in humility before the awesome majesty of the divine Creator, Who out of His infinite love has created all humanity from the same stock; exalted the gem-like reality of man; honored it with intellect and wisdom, nobility and immortality; and conferred upon man the "unique distinction and capacity to know Him and to love Him," a capacity that "must needs be regarded as the generating impulse and the primary purpose underlying the whole of creation."

We hold firmly the conviction that all human beings have been created "to carry forward an ever-advancing civilization"; that "to act like the beasts of the field is unworthy of man"; that the virtues that befit human dignity are trustworthiness, forbearance, mercy, compassion and loving-kindness towards all peoples. We reaffirm the belief that the "potentialities inherent in the station of man, the full measure of his destiny on earth, the innate excellence of his reality, must all be manifested in this promised Day of God." These are the motivations for our unshakeable faith that unity and peace are the attainable goal towards which humanity is striving. (The Universal House of Justice, *The Promise of World Peace*, ¶57–58)

BIBLIOGRAPHY

Works of Bahá'u'lláh

Epistle to the Son of the Wolf. 1st pocket-size ed. Translated by Shoghi Effendi. Wilmette, IL: Bahá'í Publishing Trust, 1988.

Gleanings from the Writings of Bahá'u'lláh. Translated by Shoghi Effendi. Wilmette, IL: Bahá'í Publishing, 2005.

The Hidden Words. Translated by Shoghi Effendi. Wilmette, IL: Bahá'í Publishing, 2002.

The Kitáb-i-Aqdas: The Most Holy Book. 1st pocket-size ed. Wilmette, IL: Bahá'í Publishing Trust, 1993.

The Kitáb-i-Íqán: The Book of Certitude. Translated by Shoghi Effendi. Wilmette, IL: Bahá'í Publishing, 2003.

Prayers and Meditations. Translated by Shoghi Effendi. 1st pocket-size ed. Wilmette, IL: Bahá'í Publishing Trust, 1987.

The Summons of the Lord of Hosts: Tablets of Bahá'u'lláh. Wilmette: Bahá'í Publishing, 2006.

The Tabernacle of Unity: Bahá'u'lláh's Responses to Mánikchí Ṣáḥib and Other Writings. Haifa: Bahá'í World Centre, 2006.

Tablets of Bahá'u'lláh revealed after the Kitáb-i-Aqdas. Compiled by the Research Department of the Universal House of Justice. Translated by Habib Taherzadeh et al. Wilmette, IL: 1988.

Works of 'Abdu'l-Bahá

'Abdu'l-Bahá in London: Addresses and Notes of Conversations. London: Bahá'í Publishing Trust, 1982.

Paris Talks: Addresses Given By 'Abdu'l-Bahá in Paris in 1911. 12th ed. London: Bahá'í Publishing, 2011.

Promulgation of Universal Peace: Talks Delivered by 'Abdu'l-Bahá during His Visit to the United States and Canada in 1912. Compiled by Howard MacNutt. 2nd ed. Wilmette, IL: Bahá'í Publishing, 2012.

Selections from the Writings of 'Abdu'l-Bahá. Compiled by the Research Department of the Universal House of Justice. Translated by a Committee at the Bahá'í World Center and Marzieh Gail. Wilmette, IL: Bahá'í Publishing, 2010.

Some Answered Questions. Haifa: Bahá'í World Centre, 2014.

"Tablet to August Forel," The Bahá'í World, vol. XV.

Works of Shoghi Effendi

Advent of Divine Justice. 1st pocket-size ed. Wilmette, IL: Bahá'í Publishing Trust, 1990.

Bahá'í Administration: Selected Messages 1922–1932. 7th ed. Wilmette, IL: Bahá'í Publishing Trust, 1974.

Citadel of Faith: Messages to America, 1947–1957. Wilmette, IL: Bahá'í Publishing Trust, 1965.

Directives from the Guardian. Wilmette, IL: Bahá'í Publishing Trust, 1973.

"The Faith of Bahá'u'lláh, A World Religion," *World Order Magazine*, volume XIII, number 7, October 1947.

God Passes By. New ed. Wilmette, IL: Bahá'í Publishing Trust, 1974.

The Promised Day Is Come. 1st pocket-size ed. Wilmette, IL: Bahá'í Publishing Trust, 1996.

The World Order of Bahá'u'lláh: Selected Letters. 1st pocket-size ed. Wilmette, IL: Bahá'í Publishing Trust, 1991.

Works of the Universal House of Justice

Messages from the Universal House of Justice, 1963–1986: The Third Epoch of the Formative Age. Compiled by Geoffry Marks. Wilmette, IL: Bahá'í Publishing Trust, 1996.

Messages from the Universal House of Justice, 1986–2001: The Fourth Epoch of the Formative Age. Compiled by Geoffry Marks. Wilmette, IL: Bahá'í Publishing Trust, 2010.

Messages from the Universal House of Justice, 1968–1973. Haifa: Bahá'í World Center, 1973.

The Promise of World Peace: To the Peoples of the World. Wilmette, IL: Bahá'í Publishing Trust, 1985.

A Wider Horizon, Selected Letters 1983–1992. West Palm Beach, FL: Palabra Publications, 1992.

To the World's Religious Leaders: A Message from the Universal House of Justice. Wilmette, IL: Bahá'í Publishing Trust, 2002.

Compilations of Bahá'í Writings

Bahá'í Prayers: A Selection of Prayers Revealed by Bahá'u'lláh, the Báb, and 'Abdu'l-Bahá. New ed. Wilmette, IL: Bahá'í Publishing Trust, 2002.

The Compilation of Compilations: Prepared by the Universal House of Justice, 1963–1990. 2 vols. Australia: Bahá'í Publications Australia, 1991.

"Economics, Agriculture, and Related Subjects," in *The Compilation of Compilations,* vol. 3. Australia: Bahá'í Publications Australia, 2000.

Lights of Guidance: A Bahá'í Reference File. Compiled by Helen Hornby. New ed. New Dehli, India: Bahá'í Publishing Trust, 1994.

"Wealth, Redistribution of." Compiled by the Research Department of the Universal House of Justice. Haifa: Bahá'í World Center, nd.

Prepared Under the Supervision of the Universal House of Justice
Century of Light. Haifa: Bahá'í World Center, 2001.
One Common Faith. Haifa: Bahá'í World Center, 2005.

Statements of the Bahá'í International Community
"A Bahá'í Declaration of Human Obligations and Rights." Presented to the first session of the United Nations Commission on Human Rights, 1 February 1947.
"Combating Racism." Statement submitted to the United Nations Second World Conference to Combat Racism and Racial Discrimination, 1 August 1983.
"Eliminating Racism." Statement to the forty-fifth session of the United Nations Commission on Human Rights Agenda Item 17 (b): Implementation of the Programme of Action for the Second Decade to Combat Racism and Racial Discrimination, 8 February 1989.
"Eradicating Poverty: Moving Forward as One." The Bahá'í International Community's Statement on Poverty, 14 February 2008.
"Global Action Plan for Social Development." Contribution to the first substantive session of the Preparatory Committee for the United Nations World Summit for Social Development, 31 January 1994.
"The Prosperity of Humankind." A statement prepared by the Bahá'í International Community Office of Public Information, Haifa, first distributed at the United Nations World Summit on Social Development, Copenhagen, Denmark, 3 March 1995.
"The Realization of Economic, Social and Cultural Rights." Written statement for the 47th session of the Sub-Commission on Prevention of Discrimination and Protection of Minorities, 31 July 1995.
"Religion as an Agent for Promoting the Advancement of Women at All Levels," introduction to *The Greatness Which Might be Theirs: Reflections on the Agenda and Platform for Action for the United Nations Fourth*

World Conference on Women: Equality, Development and Peace, 26 August 1995.

"Right to Development." Written statement to the forty-fifth session of the United Nations Commission on Human Rights. Agenda item 8: Question of the realization in all countries of the economic, social and cultural rights contained in the universal declaration of human rights and in the international covenant on economic, social and cultural rights, and study of the problems which the developing countries face in their efforts to achieve these human rights, 9 February 1989.

Statement to the 49th Session of the United Nations Commission on Human Rights, "Human Rights and Extreme Poverty." A Statement of the Bahá'í International Community, 12 February 1993.

"Statement to World Conference against Racism." A Statement of the Bahá'í International Community, 31 August 2001.

"Sustainable Communities in an Integrating World." A statement presented to the Plenary of the Second UN Conference on Human Settlements, 7 June 1996.

"Towards Full and Meaningful Participation of Persons Living in Poverty in Shaping Processes and Structures That Impact Their Lives." Bahá'í International Community's Contribution to the Report of the Special Rapporteur on Extreme Poverty and Human Rights Regarding the Participation of Persons Living in Poverty, 14 December 2012.

"Turning Point for All Nations." Statement of the Bahá'í International Community on the Occasion of the 50th Anniversary of the United Nations, October 1995.

Other Works

['Abdu'l-Bahá and Auguste Forel]. *Auguste Forel and the Bahá'í Faith.* Translated by Hélène Neri. Commentary by Peter Mühlschlegel. Oxford: George Ronald, 1978.

Abrams, M. H. *The Mirror and the Lamp: Romantic Theory and the Critical Tradition.* New York: Oxford University Press, 1953.

The Bahá'í World: A Biennial International Record, Vol II. Haifa, Israel: The Universal House of Justice, 1928.

"Social Action," A paper prepared by the Office of Social and Economic Development at the Bahá'í World Center, 26 November 2012.